T0123440

WEALTHY BY AGE THIRTY

THE GUIDE FOR YOUNG PEOPLE WHO DON'T HAVE A CLUE WHAT THEY WANT TO DO IN LIFE

This book started as a letter to my grandkids

to teach them how to become millionaires

at a young age

and have success in all things they do

THIS BOOK WILL TEACH ANYONE HOW TO EARN A STACK OF $100 BILLS
THAT WILL NEVER RUN OUT IF YOU MANAGE IT PROPERLY

By

JAMES A. GRANT

THE CHAPTERS ARE A LIST OF ONE HUNDRED PLATITUDES THAT WILL WORK IF YOU FOLLOW ANY ONE OF THEM. If you diligently follow just half of them and you are in your early twenties, I guarantee that you will actually become a millionaire by age thirty and be able to do it in an ethical manner.

If you don't accomplish it, contact me at icantfollowdirections@loser.com, or at iamsolazythatirefusetohelpmyself@patheticloser.com. You are the only person to blame for your failure. I can tell you what to do, but you have to do it.

IT IS EASIER TO BECOME WEALTHY THAN IT IS TO STAY POOR!

***

IF YOU WANT TO DO SOMETHING, YOU
WILL FIND A WAY TO DO IT.

***

IF YOU DON'T WANT TO DO SOMETHING,
YOU WILL BE ABLE TO FIND
AN EXCUSE FOR WHY YOU CAN'T DO IT

***

BECOMING RICH OR STAYING POOR IS A DECISION

WEALTHY BY AGE THIRTY
THE GUIDE FOR YOUNG PEOPLE WHO DON'T HAVE
A CLUE WHAT THEY WANT TO DO IN LIFE

iUniverse books may be ordered through booksellers or by contacting:

iUniverse
1663 Liberty Drive
Bloomington, IN 47403
www.iuniverse.com
1-800-Authors (1-800-288-4677)

ISBN: 978-1-5320-9833-8 (sc)
ISBN: 978-1-5320-9834-5 (hc)
ISBN: 978-1-5320-9832-1 (e)

Library of Congress Control Number: 2020905724

Print information available on the last page.

iUniverse rev. date: 04/14/2020

ACKNOWLEDGEMENTS

In recognition to my wonderful wife who has been at my side for fifty eight challenging but wonderful years. She has given me inspiration and strength to keep on going even when things looked pretty bleak. She has contributed equally in all of our financial decisions and dealings throughout the years. She believed in me even when I didn't believe in myself. Her steadfastness, wisdom, ethics, and strength are profound.

A wholehearted thank you to all of the many mentors that have given me bountiful advice and that have helped me enormously at every turn and shaped my destiny. I am forever grateful to them for freely giving their wisdom.

To my mother and father who instilled frugality and financial management in me by their example of efficient and careful management of every hard earned dollar they made. They could stretch a nickel into a dollar. I learned the basics of negotiation in business from them both.

To my mother-in-law and father-in-law who were a monument to ethical living and general life wisdom. My father in law was a master at seeing, understanding, and expressing the essence of any situation in the simplest and most understandable terms. Their marriage was a perfect living example of the way two people working together accomplish what four people can do if they are working alone. I thank them for their practicing example to my wife and me and to our children. I believe their long lives and lifelong marriage was their reward for the fine people they were.

INTRODUCTION

(DON'T SKIP THIS)

Do you want to become wealthy at a young enough age to enjoy it? This book will teach you how. You won't learn this in school because they don't teach it.

I started with no money, and with a little self-discipline I learned how to think like a millionaire and became a millionaire by age forty. Because I had to learn the hard way with no definitive guide in a single source like this book, I was slow. I had to dig out the information. I'm handing it to you on a silver platter. You can do it by age thirty by using what I learned the hard way. This book will show you precisely what to do and how to do it. Benefit from my mistakes.

I decided to write this book because I felt it was the best way to convey a lifetime of experience to my grandkids to absorb in easy doses as they could. It is not just for my grandkids alone, it is for any other young person. I had been jotting down important points and thoughts for them on post-it notes for a long time. After the pile got too high, I decided the only way to make sense of the information was to write this book.

This book lays out the traits in detail required to become a millionaire by age thirty in an easy to follow form that anyone can achieve. Are you willing to spend four hours or so to learn exactly how to become a millionaire? If you are, this book is for you. The traits and chapter topics are mixed around purposely in order to integrate them into other traits in different ways throughout the book.

Even though the rest of this introduction targets my own family, you might see yourself mirrored somewhere in the text, and it might be your own wakeup call to wealth. If you do make the decision to become a millionaire, you will someday face the same concern for your family as I do in the following part of the introduction. Becoming a millionaire is a decision, it is not a matter of chance.

Despite my efforts to teach my own four kids otherwise, only one and a half of them know anything about making and managing large chunks of money. Despite other positive things that they know and do, only one of my own kids fully understands and practices good financial skills. That same one also married a mate that pulls her weight and has the same goals and skill level (an essential situation). They work as a team. The half aware ones that I list is because two of the others get the concept to some degree, but are still building self-discipline skills needed to accumulate seed money. They also, still need to learn exactly how to use seed money to make their fortune grow. Those two could benefit by some further awareness. For the two that don't fully get it right now, it's never too late to start. It was never an issue of intelligence or work ethic with any of them. It is an issue of being unwilling to ask for advice from the right people and follow it. So far, they have not used the necessary financial discipline. They are financially stuck and can't grow. So far, they also haven't been willing to take the risks to make lots of mistakes and learn from each mistake. Does any of this sound like you?

The ones that don't know financial skills always resented my efforts to teach them. They don't realize just how much they don't know. Even though they are presently in their forties and fifties, they have not learned the most critical business and financial skills from anyone at all. They could observe from watching my wife and me over the years and from asking questions, but for their own personal reasons, they resisted any advice and direction and refused to emulate us. Since childhood they have openly shown no interest at all. There are also many other places they could have learned if they just didn't want to get the knowledge from me and my wife. Sounds like the classic story, doesn't it? Does any of this part sound like you?

I love them all dearly, and it hurts me to see them living their lives without learning the financial skills they so desperately need. They live their lives without the commitment and discipline which is required to become successful rather than being JUST OVER BROKE WITH A JOB and struggling every day. Most jobs mean just that: "J-just O-over B-broke". It has hurt them much more throughout their lives than they realize, and it will be devastating to them as they approach retirement. I fear that they could become one of the people bagging groceries at Walmart that is over 70 years old and can barely stand to the finish of their shift because they need a piddly job just to survive. All of my kids have a good work ethic and they are all intelligent, but some of them just don't "get it", yet. Do some people "have it" and some don't? I don't think so. Does any of this part ring a wake up bell with you?

Is the recognition and drive built into us at birth to succeed or is it a learned skill? I choose to believe that it is a learned skill and that anyone can do it. Can you?

Is some form of fear keeping them from great financial success? Is it only the unwillingness to discipline themselves that prevents them from self-motivating? Did they just resent hearing it from someone so familiar? Are they just not interested?

I believe that anyone who wants to get financial skills strongly enough will learn them by changing their habits if necessary. Could it be that they just don't want wealth and freedom BADLY enough? Maybe they just think it is too much work. Maybe they are content to be "all hat and no cattle". That is, to appear successful without actually being successful. Appearance alone is goal for some people, but this book will teach you how to do the real thing. Would you rather just appear successful or actually be successful?

THE DANGER OF INHERITED MONEY

I was well aware that if someone inherited money before they were ready, it could, and probably would, provide the means of their own self-destruction. Inherited money is dangerous.

When I was in high school, I was a lifeguard at a neighborhood swimming pool. One of my fellow lifeguards was lazy and self-secured because his father owned a large cement plant with several cement trucks. My friend told me that he didn't have to work because he knew he was going to inherit the business from his father so he wouldn't have to work. He did an absolute minimum in school and at the pool. His inheritance potential completely destroyed his drive. He didn't understand that when his father died, he was the one who would be doing all of the real work and management or the business would fall apart. I always thought that based on his attitude, he would soon be broke even if he did inherit the family business. He was basically a playboy.

I have worked with and around many wealthy and successful people. I have seen self-destruction occur many times to people when they inherit wealth before they were ready to handle it. I believe that a person is only deserving of the help of inherited money after they have learned the rules of how to handle money beforehand. If they had never learned financial skills with money they earned themselves, how would they avoid squandering the inherited money? Easy come—easy go. They would lose even more self-esteem when they realize their folly as the inherited money slips away from them in dribbles. They would be full of sorrow, of deep embarrassment, and regret. That sows the seeds of self-loathing. They need to learn financial skills from someone/anyone who can make chunks of money honorably on their own and knows how to make it grow into wealth. It doesn't matter how or where, but it is critical that they learn it.

My own kids are not my only concern. I am almost more concerned about my grandkids as they are growing into maturity. My grandkids are all at the age when the whole world is perplexing, and they are looking for a foothold in this dazzling and confusing computer driven society. I decided that the best way to introduce them to basic skills of money and business is to write it down and condense a lifetime of study of successful people, the advice of motivational experts who have been an epiphany in my own life, and the trials and many errors from my own experience. As I started jotting thoughts down, my stacks of post-it notes morphed into this book which is actually "A Letter to My Grandkids". It is to my dear grandkids that I desperately want to convey this most valuable information. I also want to share it with any other young person with the desire and grit to act on it. Do you have that desire and are you willing to act on it?

These one hundred platitudes which are the chapter titles are the lessons that I learned from long and costly experience. I personally used them all throughout my life. They are the ones I personally found the most important to becoming successful. I'm not quoting something that just sounds good. I know that each platitude really does work because they all worked for me in the real business world in several businesses. In my 70's I still use them all. I still review them all, and I study something about success from all ages of successful people almost every day. I learn from young and old alike. It is something that I believe passionately about. I believe in continually learning.

Financial success allows the freedom in life to accomplish any other success more easily. Financial success is the foundation to accomplish all further goals.

The skills to become successful in life, in business, and in financial principles really have never changed. No person owns them. Financial skills were the same in the ancient world as they are today in the internet age. They don't become obsolete like most information. They are free to anyone with the audacity to simply use them. They are so simple that many people overlook them. People tend to assume that financial success really must be something complicated or must be a secret magic formula. It isn't.

You won't learn these skills in school because they aren't taught there. School teaches you how to become a cog in the wheel. You can learn them from this book as well as numerous other scattered sources. I just hope this format will spark many successes for my grandkids and others as well. It won't work to just read the information. It won't work to commit the information to memory and even to believe in it.

You must actually ACT on the information in this book and DO it. It is a way of life. It is the backbone of a life which is successful in all things.

Success is easier than failure. Inaction is devastating. Action is fulfilling.

It helps to be miserable enough for a long enough time to make you want to succeed badly enough. Then you will actually start doing something to fix the misery just as I did. If you aren't at a desperation point yet, you just might need to wallow in it for a few more months or years until you get serious about your future.

With the vast and barely tapped opportunities on the internet, my grandkids have opportunities today that I couldn't have dreamed of as a young man. By adding these 100 workable skills and traits to that knowledge they already have now by being raised in the internet age, they can become the most powerful generation in human history. They will just have to get off their cute backsides and put the principles explained in this book to work. They must learn to recognize all of the potential money opportunities that are right under their noses every day, and then act on some of them. This is not just a book for thought. It is a book for action.

TO WHOMEVER IT MAY CONCERN:

I have concluded that the best way to transfer wealth is to make inheritances based on a gift of this vital information for my heirs. If they master this information and acquire the skills for themselves they will make their own fortunes. Whatever money might be left over for them to inherit will then be a blessing and not a curse. They will be financially mature enough only after they learn those skills to actually inherit money. This book will tell them exactly how to do it if they are mature enough and wise enough to use it. If they are not, then they likely shouldn't inherit much. Let's see what happens.

I have written this book the way I did so that after initially reading it, my grandkids and anyone else, can just open it from time to time, look at any page and immediately see something on that page that will help them.

Some of the information may seem very similar, but there is an important distinction in each lesson. One of the best things about the Holy Bible is that it is difficult to randomly open it to any page and not find a good lesson. If you give a man a fish, you feed him for a day. If you teach him how to fish, you feed him for a lifetime.

Some of the chapters in this book may seem very similar to others, but I chose to not combine those chapters because there is a subtle but distinct lesson in each one. Some concepts are mentioned repeatedly throughout the book because they integrate with what is being discussed. Repetition helps affix a concept in your mind.

At this point I would like to state one of my favorite sayings:

> "DO NOT CORRECT A FOOL OR HE WILL HATE YOU, CORRECT A WISE MAN AND HE WILL APPRECIATE YOU." (based on the Holy Bible- Proverbs9:8)

I KNOW THIS INTRODUCTION IS LONG, BUT
DON'T START READING THIS BOOK UNLESS YOU
HAVE READ THE INTRODUCTION FIRST.
THE INTRODUCTION IS THE KEY TO
THE MINDSET FOR THIS BOOK.

CONTENTS

CHAPTER 1

SUCCESS DOESN'T JUST HAPPEN—
YOU ALONE MAKE IT HAPPEN.

You must be pro-active and make opportunities happen. Opportunities are all around you. Learn to recognize and seize opportunities. You will be successful only by continually preparing yourself and by being open to opportunities. Success occurs when preparation meets opportunity. Consciously search for opportunities by talking to many successful people using a curious and positive attitude. Ask them thoughtful questions. Successful people are the kind of people who can see opportunities around them and also create them where none exist. If they perceive you as a diligent person, when they have any opportunities in mind they will consider you. The more you hang around successful people who have a good attitude, and if you have a positive attitude yourself, the more likely you will be presented with opportunity. As an example, if you were panning for gold, you wouldn't expect to find it in certain places in the stream because of strong current flow. You would go to where the speed of the current slows and drops the gold. Learn to be wherever the likelihood of opportunities is high. That would be around people who have set goals for themselves and who are improving themselves every day. The likelihood of being presented with a good opportunity is much lower around negative people who aren't really aspiring to very much. Good and bad attitudes are contagious. Keep your mind active by imagining new ways to do things and ways of marketing yourself or a product. Be open, positive and imaginative. Discuss your ideas openly so that everyone you meet understands that you are a person with defined goals who is going somewhere.

Learn to create your own opportunities by guiding conversations toward substantial things and not trivia. Don't get involved with gossip and nonsense. Create a reputation for yourself that you are to be taken seriously.

You can be fun and jovial, but conduct yourself so that people will take you seriously.

A rare opportunity happened to me when I was 15 years old. I was traveling alone on a Greyhound bus from Washington D.C. bound for Denver. An old man with a fluffy moustache and a brim hat boarded the bus and asked if he could use the empty seat next to me. I said "sure." As he sat down, he proceeded to tell me that he was going to Colorado to hunt elephants. What??? Hunt elephants!! (He did look kind of like a British big game hunter). His comment made me pause and begin to think that I was going to be riding next to a nut case all the way to Denver. I had lived all my life in Colorado and I was pretty sure that we didn't have elephants there to hunt.

The old man had one eye that was milky and non-functional. The thumb, the first two fingers, and half of his right hand were missing. His hand looked more like a claw than a hand. His jolly smile made me uncertain if he was crazy or just very friendly. As he continued talking, he told me that he worked for the Smithsonian museum in Washington D.C., and that he was the assistant curator of the division of archeology. This claim made me more suspicious than ever, and I suspected that he might be a little crazy. I thought that I was in for a very long and scary ride to Denver. As he talked more he seemed to know a lot about many different things. His conversation became more interesting as we began to talk about Indians and Indian arrowheads. The things he discussed seemed to start making sense. I loved all things Indian, and I had even experimented with chipping arrowheads and tomahawks from flint, so I was interested in what he had to say. The more he talked, the more I liked him even if he would have been crazy. I still wasn't sure about the crazy part, but we talked on for hours and he turned out to be one of the most fascinating people I had ever met. There was definitely something special about him. He finally told me that he actually was going to Colorado to dig up mammoth bones which were discovered in a rancher's artesian spring watering hole a few miles south of Denver. The expedition was for the Smithsonian with archeologists and paleontologists from the museum. That sure made more sense to me than his original claim of hunting elephants, so I let my guard down a little and started thinking that this captivating guy might be for real.

He liked my curious personality and my interest in archeology and asked me if I would like to join the expedition. He said that the government had approved funding the expedition for two years. He offered me a summer job which was usually reserved for college students studying archeology. I was under age, so technically I couldn't be hired. I was fifteen years old and the minimum age was eighteen. I found out something. When you are displaying a positive and open attitude, people will bend the rules to help you. That is an important lesson in itself. He asked for my telephone number and address just before he got off the bus when we got to Lincoln, Nebraska. He said he had to go to Lincoln to get the carryall vehicles for the expedition from the U.S. Army Corps of Engineers River Basin Survey Depot. He told me he would see me a week later in Denver. As he departed, I really didn't think I would ever see him again, but, true to his word, one week later he showed up in front of our house in a government grey River Basins Survey carryall with Dr. Waldo Wedel, the curator of the division of archeology, and said, "Pack your duffel bag and your sleeping bag, we're leaving now." It was really happening! A chance meeting turned into the opportunity of a lifetime for a curious young boy because he was open to a wild and rare opportunity. I worked for two summers on a field expedition for the prestigious Smithsonian Museum. What a fascinating experience!

We dug up seven mammoth skeletons along with many other ancient creatures and artifacts of ancient man over the two summers. That young boy rubbed shoulders and camped for months with some very interesting and substantial people. The conversations in camp at night were always stimulating. Every night was like sitting in on a college lecture. I would have never had that opportunity if I didn't talk substantially, ask questions, and remain open to possibilities while displaying the right attitude. It was a chance meeting, but I had made the most of it.

Success doesn't just happen—you have to make it happen.

CHAPTER 2

WISHING IT TO HAPPEN WON'T MAKE IT HAPPEN—IT TAKES CONSISTENT WORK TOWARD A WORTHY GOAL TO BE SUCCESSFUL.

W-I-S-H-I-N-G is for fairytales. D-O-I-N-G is what works in the real world. One of the best traits a person can have in life is what I call plodding. It means simply this: get up off your fanny and start. Just keep putting one foot in front of the other. Don't worry about mistakes or making a fool of yourself. You will make some mistakes. It is part of the game. It's the losers that don't ever try. That is why they will always be losers. Just start, and then keep putting one foot in front of the other each day, every day, and keep going. WOW! That doesn't sound like fun, does it? The thing is—it works!

In its early stages of working toward success it isn't fun, but when you start to see the progress you are making, the excitement builds and the adrenaline starts to flow as all of your dreams start to slowly emerge from the fog. You see reality manifest one small step at a time. Success first has to be conceived, then achieved. That is, you have to consciously think about what it is you want in detail, and then by working consistently one step at a time, plod toward your idea and your picture of success. There will be times when you are just tired, bored, or discouraged, but you have to keep your eye on the prize. A lot of people think they can simply want something bad enough and it will happen. Life doesn't work like that. The world is indifferent to whether you are successful or not. The world doesn't care what you want. Only your personal efforts, the skills that you learn, your ideas, and your personal interactions with other people will make you successful.

It is up to you to determine what your personal strong and weak traits are and then it is up to you alone to strengthen your weak points and capitalize on your strong points. If your weak point is talking to people, force yourself to learn how to strike up conversations at every opportunity. Learn to ask a lot of questions. It is amazing what you will learn when you punch somebody's button. Learn to look people in the eyes in an attentive way but not challenging. Everybody likes to talk about themselves and their interests. Learn to get them to talk and the conversation will be easy. Just listen. An attentive listener is in control. You should get some sort of job is sales for a time which will force you to meet and greet people. It will be uncomfortable at first, but you will soon find it easier and even enjoy it as you find that people are actually very interesting if you present yourself openly. The more successful they are, the more interesting they are to talk to because they have accomplished more. Talking to losers and lazy people isn't very interesting.

If your weak point is your appearance, look in the mirror and determine whether it is your hair style, your neatness, your cleanliness, your smile, your teeth, your posture, or just your general attitude that needs improving. Change whatever needs changing. Be constructively critical of yourself. You might even want to ask others for help who will be brutally honest with you. You don't have to be beautiful, but you can't be a slob either. If your weak trait is self-confidence, remember that by just thinking about success in a serious way will put you ahead of most of the people you meet. Most people never really get serious about achieving more than a daily existence. You are already the exception. You have already started on your journey toward being exceptional because you are already reading this information.

Develop the grit to make things happen and not just watch things happen to you.

Are you a doer or just a wisher?

Wishing it to happen won't make it happen—it takes consistent work toward a worthy goal to be successful.

CHAPTER 3

THE WORLD SETS A CEILING TO HOLD YOU EXACTLY AT THE LEVEL THAT YOU HAVE PREPARED YOURSELF FOR.

It would be pretty foolish to think that you could jump into the boxing ring with a world heavyweight champion fighter and expect to win. You couldn't realistically expect to even come out alive without years of conditioning, skill, technique training, stamina training, and strategy training. A professional fighter also needs a coach who has had more years of experience than he has had himself. Business skills, financial skills, and success skills are no different. The fighter has set a goal (say the world heavyweight title). He has trained long and hard in the gym and has many fights and many wins under his belt before he can even be considered remotely ready to challenge the present title holder. If he goes into the ring before he is fully prepared as a challenger, the titleholder will make a fool of him. He also risks serious injury.

The world will set the ceiling above you to hold you at the level you have trained or prepared for. You will not break through it to a higher level until you prepare yourself for the next higher level. That means both education (any kind) and skill level.

Always remember that your success or failure means nothing at all to the world at large. The world really doesn't care if you succeed or not, so the world isn't doing anything in particular to help you succeed. It is also doing nothing in particular to make you fail. The world is impartial to what you do with your life. What you do is completely up to you, and you alone.

SUCCESS IS WHAT HAPPENS WHEN PREPARATION MEETS OPPORTUNITY. I particularly like this saying because it puts the responsibility squarely on your own shoulders. Many people miss opportunities because they aren't prepared to recognize opportunities. Obscure opportunities come in so many forms and come at the most inopportune times. If the people around you know that you have developed the skills and knowledge to handle a new responsibility, or business opportunity, they will present it to you. The more substantial facts and skills that you know, the more valuable you are. Most men and women are worth about the same from the neck down. That is, the only thing that makes you into a much more valuable person is the skills you have learned and how effective you can apply them to help someone else attain their needs or goals.

You may have a brilliant mind and be able to invent things, you may be able to communicate ideas well, you may have a trade or craft skill, you may have a sports skill, you may have a teaching skill, or you may be a fantastic salesman. There are thousands of skills that can set you apart from the crowd and give you the necessary earning power to earn your seed money to start really making serious money in any number of businesses. Maybe the skill itself that you have is so outstanding that you will be one of those very few people who can make millions just on that skill alone. An example of that would be wonderful singer or a basketball star. In any case, the preparation or training you do is what will set you apart from the masses. Learn and then earn. First, you will just earn with your labor and skills, and then you will need to learn another key skill. That all important skill is to know how to put seed money to work to earn even more money by creating passive income. More on that later, but remember the term "passive income"

The world sets a ceiling to hold you exactly at the level that you have prepared yourself for.

CHAPTER 4

YOU WILL GET WHAT YOU WANT FINANCIALLY IF YOU HELP ENOUGH OTHER PEOPLE GET WHAT THEY WANT.

Zig Ziglar is one of the best motivational speakers in my opinion. He conveyed several basic principles, including this one, to the audience in a positive thinking seminar that I attended in my twenties. I still listen to the tapes I bought from him at the seminar I attended fifty years ago. Those tapes, as well as tapes from several other motivational speakers have been invaluable to me over the decades in business. As a regular reinforcement, you should develop the habit of studying many different motivational speakers on a regular basis. Those people are in the business of conveying invaluable life experiences to you. A combination of several of them will definitely guide you to success. Each one has their own specific lessons. By listening to their advice, you will run across a few very specific sayings that speak directly to you and will click for you personally. They will become the roadmap of your particular successes.

Today, numerous programs are free on You Tube including most of the great speakers. Also, numerous other people who have followed their advice, will then share their own experiences becoming a testimonial. Make it a habit of watching this kind of information rather than the silly, mindless entertainment of people doing stupid things, endless cat videos, or of filling your mind with useless trivia.

Analyze the statement in this chapter title and think about it. If you help other people with a service or product that they want, they will literally beat a path to your door to exchange their money for what you are offering. Another way to say it is "Find a need and then fulfill it!" That sentence is the basis of all successful businesses. That is what Henry Ford did with his cheap mass produced Model T. It is what Rockefeller did with oil. It is what Bill Gates did with Microsoft. It is what Steve Jobs did with the I Phone. It is what millions of small business owners do every day all around the world by bringing all kinds of products to you. Just a few decades ago, the revolutionary way to market was in the Montgomery Ward catalogue and Sears and Roebuck catalogue with black and white sketches which brought thousands of items to city people and rural people all across America. Today it is the internet, and it is instant. The internet is the most powerful tool in history!

On the gold fields of California in the 1850's, only a very small percentage of the miners got rich from finding gold. The people who made the most money were the thousands of people who supplied the miners with shovels, gold pans, hardware, food, clothing, laundry services, whiskey and entertainment. The famous Levi Strauss jeans were a product which was spawned from a need of miners. They needed tough, durable canvas pants with rivets at the seams so that the pockets wouldn't tear out when they shoved jagged ore samples into their pockets.

The principal of helping other people get what they want is so simple that it is easy to overlook. Learn to think in terms of fulfilling a want or a need. There are literally millions of brand new ideas that nobody has thought of yet and any one of them could be that multibillion dollar idea such as Facebook. If you are constantly looking for ideas and you train yourself to think in terms of filling a need for other people, you will recognize opportunities when you run into them.

Opportunities are everywhere. The internet gives you instant access to millions of people all over the world. That single factor makes it the most powerful tool ever invented. Ideas, processes, services, and products can be made instantly available to millions of people worldwide with a keystroke.

You will get what you want financially if you help enough other people get what they want.

CHAPTER 5

THE WORLD DOESN'T OWE YOU A DAMN THING.

One of the surest ways to alienate the people around you and assure your failure is to have the attitude that the world owes you a living. If you are alive and breathing, you are responsible for everything that you do. You are also responsible for the things that you should do but don't do.

There is a common political attitude in our present time that the government owes you something just because you were lucky enough to be born. Why does the government owe you anything? One of the best things you can do for yourself and for your country is to be motivated to success. If you aren't motivated to success, you are wasting your life and are a drain on your country.

Working at a job is the first step in building wealth. It is where you will earn your seed money for bigger things and easier money. I am absolutely disgusted when someone says "I can't find a job. I'm too young and I can't get a work permit, or, I'm too old and nobody will hire me." Baloney!!! If you want work, there are always jobs to be had. You just have to be creative enough to find them. I never went for more than a few days without a job because I never gave up. I really wanted to work because I had to work. I knew that if I didn't work, I would starve. A lot of people want a paycheck, but not a job or responsibility. I have always known that it was nobody else's responsibility to give anything to me.

Some of my grandchildren's parents have repeatedly told me that their kids can't get a job because they don't have a work permit. That same work permit was required when I was a boy, but that never stopped me from bypassing big businesses and corporations to ferret out the thousands of small businesses and individuals who wanted a little dependable help anywhere they could find it. I have heard the word "resume" so many times that I want to throw up. Kids don't need resumes to get an entry level job. That comes much later when you have a list of credentials and work experience that means something. Starting means just that—ground level entrance level W-O-R-K.

Among early jobs that I did as a young boy include mowing lawns, shoveling snow, weeding flower beds, hand watering lawns during restricted water droughts, collecting pop bottles, selling flower seeds, making cool aid and lemonade and selling it in a stand, buying eggs in quantity and selling them from a wagon that I pulled door to door, manufacturing banjo necks in a small banjo factory, lifeguarding at a swimming pool, selling magazine subscriptions, pumping gasoline, working in a small dairy store as a soda jerk, working as a bouncer at a drive in theater, dehorning cattle, working as a fry cook, and working in a hobby shop. Not a single one of those jobs required a resume. Several jobs I got came from saying to the person "I'll work for free for a few hours and if you like what I do, then hire me! If you don't like my work, you just got a few hours for free." It worked. They always hired me when they saw that I was a good worker.

My parents didn't believe in allowances. If my brother and I wanted any money, we had to earn it. My brother was even more creative than I was for creating opportunities as a boy. At age twelve, he wanted a job selling newspapers so much that he pestered the small newspaper people every day. He was successful after several return visits, each time telling them that he was a year older. They finally got so tired of telling him "no" that they finally let him sell newspapers. They were so amused after several days when he painted on a moustache with a pen to make himself look older, that they couldn't refuse such a determined young man.

What it takes is DETERMINATION. Don't take "no" for an answer. Leave your pride at home and keep going back until the people you are talking to will see that you are dedicated to your success. That kind of determination is what will make you stand out and make you wealthy. Few people have that kind of grit. Those are the winners.

Dejectedly walking away when someone first tells you "NO!" is the first clue that you will ultimately fail because you are not determined enough. You will encounter "no's" many times before you will get a single "yes". I learned that lesson when I was six years old and sold flower and garden seeds door to door. There are over seven billion people on our planet. The very few who have the sheer belief in themselves and the moxie to persevere after many rejections are the ones who will become successful. Rejection is the one thing I learned to overcome when doing door to door selling. It takes a very small percentage of "yes" answers to make a very successful day.

Most people are lazy, and many are just clueless. Most resumes are thrown in the trash can, and the chances of people who just take "no" for an answer are also thrown into the trash can. You have to stand out and prove yourself somehow before people will take you seriously. This applies even more before you are old enough to have an established track record with work experience. It is up to you to be creative enough to stand out from the crowd. Society teaches us to be followers and to be worker bees. You have to be willing to stand out from the crowd and not be just a follower.

I was recently told a story that really spoke to me. It was about a mentor who was attempting to teach a young student how to become rich. The young man had come to him with a naïve' general statement that he desired to become rich, expecting the mentor to have some magic formula that would instantly make it come true for him. The mentor had the young man meet him at a place near a river at sunrise the next day. When I heard the story, I thought the mentor was just trying to see if the young man would get off his fanny early in the morning to even meet with him. Not so. He had an even more important lesson in mind. When the young man showed up the next day at the crack of dawn, the mentor wasn't there. The young man waited and waited. After a while, the young man began to think that a trick was being played on him. Just then he caught sight of the mentor coming down the path to the river. The mentor approached the young man, patted him on the back. He said "Young man, how badly do you want to become rich?" to the young man. "Oh, very badly! I want it more than anything." replied the young man. "We'll see. Come with me.", replied the old mentor as he smiled and led the young man out chest deep into the cold river. The mentor suddenly grabbed the young man, dunked his head under the water and held him there until the young man thought he was going to drown. After the young man had gasped, thrashed and kicked in desperation for several seconds and in fear of his life, the old mentor pulled him out of the water and let him catch his breath. Staring sternly directly into his face, the mentor said sternly to the young man "Until you desire to be rich as much as you desired that breath of air as I held you under water in your panic, you will not become rich!"

Getting rich and being successful ain't for sissies. If you don't presently have the determination and discipline to stay the course already, then develop it. Toughen up and develop some grit. Determine that you will toughen your resolve so that you will keep forging ahead when there are obstacles in the way. Keep looking at all problems you encounter from different perspectives until you do find the perfect words to say, the right action to take, the right idea to pursue, or the one enlightenment which will solve the problem. One of the traits of all successful people is that they identify any problem, then solve it logically and creatively. Life can be defined as a continual cascade of changing problems to be solved. Those people who learn how to face and deal with problems are the most successful in all things. You will be successful if you face and solve each problem.

UNTIL SOMEONE IS MISERABLE ENOUGH FOR LONG ENOUGH, THEY WON'T HAVE THE DETERMINATION TO BECOME EITHER SUCCESSFUL OR WEALTHY. Until you want it as bad as the breath of life itself, it will elude you. It won't come to you just because you think the world owes you something.

I personally think that everyone living should have to experience true desperation for at least two years. I have done so for several years, and I think it is one of the best ways to build unshakeable grit and resolve. The kind of grit and resolve that won't allow you to quit when things get tough.

The world doesn't owe you a damn thing.

CHAPTER 6

IF YOU DON'T HAVE A DEFINED DIRECTION OR GOAL, YOU WILL NEVER GET THERE.

All journeys begin with one single step. You might assume that you will make that first step with your foot. It is not with your foot, it is with your mind. You have to determine where you want to go before you can even remotely know which direction to start. Most people actually wander through life with very fuzzy and general goals like "I want to become rich.", or "I want to become successful.", or "I want to become a rock star.", or "I want a good education." All of those admirable goals are far too general and not at all specific. A general goal defeats you before you get started because it is too broad and doesn't narrow down the precise step that you need to take next. It breeds inaction.

Let's use the example of a road trip. You are in Los Angeles, California and you decide that you want to visit the Metropolitan Museum in New York City. Your first decision is to choose which way to turn when you walk out your front door, and then you will make thousands of minor decisions and corrections as you make each turn as you drive. You work your way through the highways to get out of Los Angeles, then out of California, then each state as you snake your way to New York City. Obviously, you will need some kind of road map and a specific plan to know where to turn at every stage of the trip. Without a roadmap you will just aimlessly wander around. Your roadmap is your specific plan in detail. There are infinite numbers of ways to get there, but you must decide on one of them and stick to it as long as it serves to get you closer to your destination. If you keep changing your route, it will slow down your trip and waste time on your trip or waste years on your journey of life. Make a decision and stick to it AS LONG AS THAT PARTICULAR ROUTE IS LOGICAL AND GETTING YOU TO YOUR GOAL. There will certainly be unforeseen things that will delay you like road closures or bad weather. As soon as it becomes apparent that you took a wrong turn and are going the wrong direction, back up to your last decision point, correct your course and keep on forging ahead. Eventually, with determination, you will arrive in New York City and then you can navigate to the museum. You will have reached your specific goal. Navigating through life is no different. If you just say "I think I'll just start heading east". I guarantee you that you will take much longer to get to New York City than it would if you carefully chose which road was on the most direct route and made the necessary corrections. When the plan is too general it is inefficient. Without a specific plan, you will make many more mistakes and you will travel more miles to get there. You will just as likely end up in Florida as you will in New York. You will fail to reach your goal without being specific. The same goes for the journey of life.

If the people you hang around don't have specific goals, that general and unfocused thinking will rub off on you. Avoid people who don't have specific and worthy goals in life. Surround yourself with people who are doing challenging and worthy things.

If you don't have a defined direction or goal, you will never get there.

CHAPTER 7

THE WAY YOU THINK DETERMINES YOUR SUCCESS.

If you think small, you will only accomplish small things. Have the audacity to think big and do big things. Take small consistent steps toward your goals every single day. Consciously ask yourself every day "What have I done this very day toward my goals?" Physically write anything you have done toward your goals in a notebook every single day. It should be short and exact. Just a word or two will do. It will force you into the habit of focusing on where exactly that you are going and will remind you daily that you are making progress. This habit will start to train you to think like a millionaire. In order to become a millionaire you have to think like one. The likelihood of becoming a millionaire without consistent goal setting and plodding toward those goals is about as likely as being struck by lightning. It can happen, but very seldom does. A recent news broadcast says that there are 15 million millionaires in the world and there are over 7 billion people. That is 1 millionaire per 466 people on the planet, or roughly 0.2 % (two tenths of one percent) of the total population. Do you have what it takes? If not, are you willing to improve yourself to learn what it takes? I have also Googled this claim and it is roughly accurate according to them.

If you fill your mind with silly and inconsequential facts and entertain yourself constantly with aimless You Tube videos or social media dribble you will literally rot your deductive reasoning power. You Tube is one of the most powerful free educational tools in the world----if and only if you watch the right kind of videos. You can spend an hour a day watching silly people do silly and useless things, or you can take that same hour and watch some highly useful and accurate videos on business principles and success traits. Watching a cute cat video now and then is fine, but use the bulk of the time online and on You Tube learning something that will be useful to your future. I spend at least an hour a day watching biographies of successful people, world leaders, and motivational speakers and I am 74 years old. I do that even after I have already made my fortune. We are never too old to learn from everyone else. Some of the best videos I have watched are made by very young people who became aware of success principles very early in life. Much younger than I became aware.

Teenagers who are already millionaires by understanding the internet and starting businesses are teaching me about this new and powerful venue. I am constantly amazed at their ingeniousness. How are they different from you? Why can't you be one of them? Somewhere along the line they simply put an idea together and persisted until they brought it into reality. You can do it, too

Poor people have very specific thinking habits and spending habits. Rich people have a very different set of thinking and spending habits. Poor people remain poor because they are unwilling to rationally examine the real reason they are poor. They are not poor because nobody gave them any money. They are poor because they don't take the responsibility of why they remain poor and change the way they think. You will always remain poor if you don't learn to handle your money wisely and learn to train yourself to become of more value to others. Our economy is designed to tempt us all to overspend on nonsense at every turn. That goes for cars, food, clothes, drinks, recreational drugs, and trinkets. We are promised that every product they show us will bring instant gratification. Instant gratification is a Siren's song. If you can conquer the need for instant gratification, you will be on your way to becoming rich and successful. Successful people always have their eye on the long term goals. The rich didn't think about partying on Friday night. They refused to spend their money on living large for a few hours to bolster their ego. They treat themselves to a small pleasure now and then so they can do anything they want to do in the future. They delayed their gratification. They can splurge on living large later, when they have made significant excess money. Most millionaires I know are still frugal with their money even after they have made plenty of it because they have learned that it is much wiser to live below your means than at or above your means. They have the personal satisfaction that they could pay cash for a Ferrari, but they don't buy it because it isn't the wisest choice for them.

Most of the people who live large are wannabees. There are very few at the very top of the scale of multimillionaires and billionaires that have so much money that they can be foolish and still be ok. I know nothing about that echelon of people. My job in this book is to make millionaires out of my grandchildren, not billionaires. There is no practical reason for anyone to have a billion dollars except a pathologically inflated ego and a need for excessive power. I do know by personal experience that you can become a millionaire honestly with diligence, but I haven't studied any billionaires who hadn't had some hint of ruthlessness in their history.

Compete only with yourself and don't worry about what other people are doing. Think about how you can improve yourself and let other people do what they will.

The way you think determines your success.

CHAPTER 8

YOU WILL FIND THE REAL SOURCE OF YOUR TROUBLES BY LOOKING IN THE MIRROR.

It is easy to blame everything that is wrong in your life on someone else. The sign of real immaturity in a person is to listen to them deflect the blame for something they have done. They also make constant excuses for everything they have not done that they are supposed to do. If you find yourself making excuses automatically to save face, you are immature. Until you can look in the mirror and point your finger at yourself, blaming yourself squarely for your situation, you will remain an incomplete person. Real successes will elude you.

If you are broke, it is because you haven't learned how to earn and manage money. If you are uneducated, you haven't put in the time to read and study. If you are unaccomplished in personal things, it is because you are lazy. If you are slovenly it is because you haven't learned proper grooming habits. Your personal discipline is poor. The fault lies with you. The only person you should be blaming is the person staring back at you when you look at yourself in the mirror. All of us find some situations in life that are out of our control. It is a simple thing to study any situation and lay the plans to solve whatever the problem is. Your reaction should be to directly identify it, attack it, and solve it. Look at any deficiency you have in this area as a problem to identify and to solve. If something is wrong in your life it is up to you to fix it.

Let's say that you were born into poverty. That fact wasn't your fault, but what are you going to do about it? Many people would just whine about their condition and expect someone else to help them.

A person bound for success will say to themselves "I don't like being poor and I vow to work myself out of my poverty." They spend their time diligently figuring out a way to hustle at any honest work. They begin to save their seed money from their initial meager earnings, fully knowing that if they don't give up, they will eventually have enough money to get a start. They live below their means so that the excess will accumulate. Then they study any source and talk with many of the right people to get themselves pointed in the right direction.

Many of the most motivated people I have ever met were dirt poor when they were young. That dire poverty is what motivated them. They were so miserable in their poverty that they committed themselves with all their might to never be poor again. They looked in the mirror and said "I'm not stupid and I am willing to work. I absolutely will not accept poverty as my lot in life!" They could have easily given up, but they had the grit to forge ahead in small and manageable steps to learn all of the steps to success. They didn't blame fate, the world, the government, or make excuses for why they were poor. They just got off their butt and did what it took to change their situation. Successful people have no tolerance for people who whine around about everything that happens to them and won't help themselves. Successful people respect and help others who show that they are working toward success. Note that I say working, not wishing.

Make it a practice to glance into the mirror and recognize your own reflection for what it is—the person that is responsible for your troubles. That reflection is also the one person in the world that can and will fix those troubles. Don't hate yourself for being your own worst enemy. We all start there. Just be willing to cooperate with yourself to work as a team to think through how you will solve each difficulty as it arises.

One trait that the world loves is a person who is big enough to admit his mistakes openly and quickly. Nothing garners confidence in a person more than someone who can learn from mistakes. We all make them. Learn from your own mistakes and also study other people's mistakes and learn from those, too. Show me a person that doesn't make mistakes and I'll show you a person that doesn't do anything. The most successful people make the most mistakes, but they learn from each mistake and don't repeat it. It is called personal responsibility. Benjamin Franklin is quoted as saying "Experience keeps a dear school, but a fool will learn in no other." He means that you don't have to make every mistake yourself. You should be observant and listen to good advice from people who have already made the mistake.

You will find the real source of your troubles by looking in the mirror.

CHAPTER 9

THE SINGLE MOST IMPORTANT TRAIT YOU CAN HAVE IS TO TAKE ALL RESPONSIBILITY FOR YOUR ACTIONS OR INACTIONS.

Personal responsibility defines a true leader. Personal responsibility is essential to correct thinking which will guide you to all avenues of success. You will discover many things that you will need to learn and do to attain success in any pursuit. You will also need to be aware that there are also many things that you cannot do if you want long term success.

This could be a very long chapter, but the next paragraph is all encompassing and is a truckload of responsibility. Read it over and over and let it sink in.

Always act with honor and integrity. Always act with good intentions. Always be diligent. Always be on time. Always be true to your word. Always honor the promises you make, but make very, very few of them. Promises are easy to make and sometimes very hard to keep. Always tell the truth. Always admit when you are wrong. Always be willing to say "I'm sorry" and mean it. Always pay your debts. In short, take full responsibility for your actions.

It is sometimes personally satisfying to tell someone off (such as an employer), but doing so simply insures that you have made an enemy that will probably never help you in the future. Instead, learn to always be gracious and leave a good impression in all of your dealings. You won't always get the same thing in return from people, but they are their own problem. You will be amazed throughout life how many people you run into from your distant past, and they will all have an impression of you based on how responsible you were.

Inaction is when you know you should do something, but you don't. An example is, if you wanted to enroll in a school or in a class and you fool around and don't get it done. You are responsible for the potential life changing consequences of your inaction. I did that once and it affected me for years to come. I left the long enrollment line in a college class to get back to my job on time for an important technical trial we were doing on a production line. It wouldn't have mattered if I was late for the trial, but by not enrolling, I didn't get into an important chemistry course. It was a mistake that I always regretted.

Control your temper. You can't think rationally when you are angry. Anger clouds your judgement. People who use their temper as a tool are actually using inaction of personal control. Nothing destroys teamwork any quicker than out of control tempers. Learn to express yourself with well thought out explanations, not anger. The inaction of not controlling your anger can be disastrous for your future.

As you go through life, there will definitely be a few people who simply don't like you for whatever reason. At different times those people will work with you, under you, or over you. If you conduct yourself with personal responsibility, they will respect you even if they don't like you.

The single most important trait you can have is to take all responsibility for your actions or inactions.

CHAPTER 10

SUCCESS BREEDS SUCCESS.

When you are successful achieving one goal, the next one becomes easier. Apply what you learned to the next goal and be successful at that. Each time gets a little easier.

Break down the steps toward all of your goals into small manageable bites so they are easy to handle mentally and physically. There is a technique I learned in hiking that trains you to automatically change the length of your steps to adjust for the steepness of the hill. When you are on flat ground, it is easy to take long steps and cover a lot of ground in a short time. As the ground in front of you becomes steeper, you simply adjust the length of your steps shorter and shorter as the hill gets steeper and steeper to sort of shift gears so it reduces the strain on your body. You can go the distance without wearing out. By taking shorter steps, you still move forward and upward without becoming winded.

Learn to think in small steps. Write those steps down. It automatically gives you an outline of exactly what you will need to do next. After you do this for a while, your thinking will become more logical. You will begin to automatically start to attack every single problem or goal in your life with clarity with ease. You will see that the goal you first viewed as an impossible mountain to climb becomes just another little hill. After you conquer a few of those hills, you will realize that life is just a continuous stream of problems to be solved. Each success gets easier. The high that you get by seeing yourself as a repeated winner gives you the confidence to accomplish even more. The people who learn to solve problems logically are the successful ones.

The people who constantly complain are simply people who have never developed their problem solving skills. They are the losers. They will always complain that they are victims of some force beyond their control. They will never go anywhere in life until they take personal responsibility for their actions and learn to solve their problems. The more successes you have, the more successes you will continue to have because you will get more efficient at solving problems.

It is important to make the point again that the more you hang out with successful people and people who are bound for success, the more their attitudes and habits will rub off on you. The opposite is also true. The more you hang out with naysayers, complainers, and people without goals, the more those traits will rub off on you.

SHOW ME WHO YOUR FRIENDS ARE AND I WILL SHOW YOU WHAT YOUR FUTURE WILL BE. It is an absolute certainty that you will become a mirror of the company you keep.

Success breeds success.

CHAPTER 11

SUCCESSFUL PEOPLE ARE USUALLY GLAD TO GIVE THEIR ADVICE TO THOSE WHO WILL LISTEN AND DO, BUT THEY HAVE NO PATIENCE FOR THOSE THAT WON'T.

There is an old expression "You can lead a horse to water, but you can't make him drink." It is a tragedy of the human condition that each generation seems to need to make the same mistakes over and over again. The reason? Most people don't observe and learn from the mistakes and advice of other qualified people.

Humanity hasn't advanced as a species since the dawn of civilization. Why? It is because in each generation, young people as a group have always thought that their own generation has all the answers. It is true that knowledge itself doubles at an astounding rate, but what is referred to as "common sense" is in no greater supply than it was thousands of years ago. We have all heard about "common sense", but just what is it?

One of my sons once said to me that he just wanted to get to the finish line without going through the difficulties of the journey to get there. He wanted for me to give him some magic formula that would allow him to become rich and accomplished. He said "I want what you have, but I don't want to have to do all of the stuff you did to get there." That isn't how the world works.

When I was still a young boy, my father told me that when he was young, he wanted to be a millionaire playboy. He said that he had the playboy part all figured out, but he didn't have the millionaire part figured out yet. Even though he became a very good worker in his adulthood, as a kid he had erroneously looked for that same free ride that my son looked for. It isn't how the world works.

The world is speckled with successful people who are grateful for their own success and are willing to freely share their wisdom with anyone who shows a serious interest in becoming successful themselves. I have personally been mentored by famous authors, businessmen, engineers, doctors, judges, politicians, numerous professionals, my wife, my mother, dad and other relatives, numerous friends and even an enemy or two. If you openly and repeatedly ask the most qualified people you know for advice, they will give it to you for free. If you don't know any qualified people, find them. Seek them out and simply say "I am attempting to learn about--------, will you tell me something that will help me." I have NEVER been turned down, and the advice they offered was almost always worth considering. Never forget that you can learn something from everybody.

The wisdom of taking advice varies. You should be sure to take advice about any particular subject from someone who is qualified to give it based on their knowledge and experience in that field. Knowledge in one field doesn't automatically translate to knowledge in another field. A lot of PhDs automatically think that their deep knowledge of one narrow field makes them experts in other unrelated fields. It doesn't! Advice from some friends is burdened with not being completely honest with you. Advice from people who are jealous of you can send you down the wrong path. Just consider the source of the person giving it to you and consider what their motives are. I rely strongly on advice from successful people who have nothing to gain personally by giving it.

Common sense is what you do with the good advice that is given to you. Do you ignore it because you are already so smart? Do you think about it and then use your limited experience to override it? Do you blindly follow it? Do you consider it as limited knowledge because nobody knows everything? Do you weigh advice from many different sources and find the common threads of truth and apply them? Which choice seems the most logical? If you have common sense you will instinctively know how to use advice best.

Successful people are usually glad to give their advice to those who will listen and do, but they have no patience for those that won't.

CHAPTER 12

DON'T TAKE FINANCIAL ADVICE FROM ANYONE WHO IS NOT ALREADY A MILLIONAIRE.

Many people are full of financial advice and give it before they ever accomplish any degree of financial success for themselves. They might even have your best interest at heart, but they don't know what they are talking about.

Doesn't it make sense to listen to those who have already made and held onto at least a million dollars for themselves? Why on earth would you want to take financial advice from someone who lives paycheck to paycheck? If they are so smart, then why aren't they rich already? They are just getting by because they either listened to the wrong advice themselves, they never developed financial self-discipline themselves, or they didn't bother to study financial principles. Financial principles are not taught in school. Information about financial principles best comes from the people who have studied them, learned to apply them, and are willing to share that information. They are the millionaires. There are variations in their methods, but each has things you can learn. The best thing to do is to study several of them and compare.

In time past, you could simply save money and put it in the bank. Interest would compound over time. Ultimately over decades, you could become wealthy. Those days are gone.

The banking system and the Federal Government are in a relationship that manipulates anyone who is not already rich. Due to exceedingly low interest rates and to due to inflation that is actually much higher that the official reports indicate, just saving money actually results in a loss in buying power. Every day, every dollar you have is worth a little less than it was the day before. The actual buying power of a dollar in your pocket today is only worth about three cents of buying power in 1920. I was a boy in 1950 and a dime then would buy about what a dollar will buy today. The same dime candy bar in 1950 costs a full dollar today. In order to outpace inflation and the loss of buying power, you have to learn to leverage your money. That will be discussed in more detail in the next chapter and in later chapters.

At different times as my kids were growing up, I hypothetically asked them "If somebody gave you $10,000 in cash, exactly what would you do with it?" I was actually testing them to see if they had developed any financial maturity yet. Unfortunately, they answered with what they thought I wanted to hear. They knew that I thought spending it was the wrong answer, so they said "save it". The right answer is to put it to work at a higher yield than inflation. Only one of my four kids went on to learn good financial skills. If the others ever get over their hang-ups, they can learn the financial skills that will secure their futures, too. They will be able to stop laboring for every dollar and learn the biggest secret to wealth—passive income.

People who haven't actually earned large chunks of money, accumulate large chunks of money, and dealt in large chunks of money, think that if you squirrel money away and save it, that it will somehow magically grow in actual value. They simply don't have a full understanding of money and how it works.

Again, it was once partially true that you could just labor for many years and save yourself rich. No longer! Lightning fast stock trading computers, manipulated stock markets, manipulated bond markets, manipulated commodities markets, and crooked politicians have modified that fact. Today it takes the understanding of the power of chunks of cash money, an intricate understanding of the huge power of the internet, and innovative new ways of looking at all processes and things that create the leverage necessary to generate real wealth through passive income in order to get rich. Passive income is one of the most important principles you will ever learn. I'll talk more about that a little later.

Don't take financial advice from anyone who is not already a millionaire.

CHAPTER 13

YOU CAN'T SAVE YOURSELF RICH.
NOT WITH INFLATION.

Inflation is not accidental. It is the horrible and insidious creation of governments to steal quietly from all of its citizens. Let me explain. Governments need a steady supply of money to operate. The Federal government supplies services such as a military for defense, a postal service, interstate regulating agencies, and interstate facilities such as interstate highways. State and local governments supply policing services, school systems, traffic control grids, fire and rescue services, local regulatory services, and local utility regulation. As people want more from their governments, new agencies, services, laws, and facilities are created. They have to be paid for with taxes. Each group of people has its own pet projects. As politicians try to cater to anyone who will get them re-elected, they make promises to give about everything to any group they happen to be talking to at the moment so they will be re-elected. This is true in all governments. Raising taxes is always highly unpopular and politicians at the Federal level have found a really sneaky method of getting around all of that unpleasantness. Politicians have discovered that if they just allow the Federal Reserve Bank to print more and more paper dollars there will be plenty of money for all of their pet projects. The catch is that all of those extra dollars that are added into the economy actually dilute the buying power of the dollars that are already out there. The government issues I.O.Us in the form of Treasury bills to cover the borrowing of more and more dollars. It becomes debt that future generations pay back. In actual fact they know that it will never be paid back and the private bankers will ultimately own our country outright. Our country is presently 23 trillion dollars in debt and it is printing more and borrowing more every year. Inflation can only end when the governmental budgets are balanced and the politicians stop spending more and promising more than they take in through taxes.

An important history lesson:

The systemic reason for inflation to be in our financial system is as follows:

In 1913 a secret group of financiers met at an island off the Georgia coast called Jekyll Island. They secretly and illegally ramrodded a bill through Congress to establish what they called the Federal Reserve Bank. They liked the name because it sounds like it is an official government institution. It has absolutely nothing to do with the Federal Government. Instead, it is a consortium of private bankers that conspired to print and loan money to the Federal Government and charge interest on it. This was all done illegally, but the financiers were so powerful that it has never been formally challenged. Challenging them is like picking a fistfight with Mike Tyson. They are almost free from oversight. They charge interest to the Federal Government (which is indirectly charged to all U.S. taxpayers). They continue to print more and more excess money each year with nothing at all to back the money. From its formation, our government printed its own money and paid no interest on it. It bought up gold and silver as it was discovered. The treasury held the actual gold and silver metal in vaults to insure the fundamental value of the paper currency by backing it with the silver or gold metal. President Nixon took us off the gold standard because we were spending too much money and we had to pay for the Vietnam War. France started demanding debt payment in gold as our paper gold certificates promised. That was the beginning of the extra inflation. Later we also dropped the silver standard so that now our money is actually what is known as "fiat currency". It can be manipulated by simply printing extra piles of money for free. As the money is distributed through the economy, it dilutes the buying power of all the previously earned money in everyone's bank accounts. It isn't backed by anything. Since then, the printing of excess paper money has run amuck. If you would really like to understand the Federal Reserve System in detail, read the book entitled "The Creature from Jekyll Island" by G. Edward Griffin. It is over 500 pages describing detailed workings of the Federal Reserve System. I strongly advise you to read it.

The way the Federal Reserve System prints increasing amounts of money is like having a glass of Coca Cola and pouring glass after glass of water into it until it loses all of its taste and value. The value of money is diluted in the same way. The Federal Reserve admits to printing an excess of around 3 percent extra money each year, but in actuality, it has printed trillions more of extra dollars beyond that percentage. That is where additional hidden inflation comes from. The real and actual inflation rate and reduction of buying power of the dollar is somewhere around 15 percent per year.

That in a nutshell is why you can't save yourself rich. Your money loses buying power quicker than it can gain by earning interest in a bank. Many Congressmen are so uneducated financially that they don't even know that inflation is not accidental. It is a horrible and hideous creation of governments designed to steal quietly from citizens over and above charging them legitimate taxes which are necessary. Governments need a steady supply of money to operate, but systemic inflation is the most insidious form of theft from private citizens.

The stock market average yield over many decades is around 10 percent. Unless you either are trading on secret inside information (which is illegal) or you are exceedingly lucky, you will lose 5 percent of your buying power on the money you invest in the stock market. It looks like you are making money but you are actually losing buying power. You also have to pay taxes on the numerical profits even though your actual buying power is less.

The instant stock trading platforms have also rigged the game so that stocks, bonds, forex currency markets, commodities markets, and phony derivative markets are controlled by the super-rich financier bankers and their super computers. The average investor is simply raw meat to be gobbled up by their manipulations. I once had serious money in those markets. They cleaned me out in a flash with their many forms of manipulations. It took me awhile to figure out exactly what had happened. It was a very costly lesson. With the present conditions in the stock markets, your actual odds are similar to gambling in a Las Vegas casino. Dealing in those markets for anything less than the assets and influence of a billionaire (with a "b") is a fool's errand. Billionaires are a different breed from millionaires.

Billionaires usually maintain their power by buying influence and control with their money and thereby insure their position of power in the world. They pay a disproportionately small percentage of taxes because the laws are made by the super-rich and for the super-rich. The wealthiest corporations and individuals in America pay little or no taxes into a system that allows them to practice their rampant greed.

The people who tell you that you can get rich by saving in banks by compounding interest have obviously don't know that inflation also compounds just as interest does. If actual inflation (not reported inflation) is larger than interest, you will actually lose spending power on the money you are saving.

Saving cash in a bank for long periods without putting it to work in investments is a sure way to make your fortune dwindle in spending power.

You can't save yourself rich. Not with inflation.

CHAPTER 14

LEARN TO THINK IN LARGE CHUNKS OF MONEY.

Most people let small amounts of money slip away from them in numerous ways. My brother couldn't pass up a peanut machine, pop machine or gumball machine without putting a coin in it. It was completely wasted money. He was a very innovative worker with a very good work ethic, but he never learned how to manage his money. If we went to several stops, he would spend a couple of dollars by the end of the day. Today, kids feed their coins into video game machines the same way and spend far too much on the latest electronic gadget or cellphone.

If you have goals in your mind for your life, you will start examining where every cent of your money goes. Develop the habit of physically writing down where every cent of your money goes and you will automatically find out where you are being foolish. You shouldn't deny yourself all pleasures, but keep the pleasure spending to a minimum until you are rich. You will either be frugal when you are building your fortune, or you will become older and live paycheck to paycheck with no financial freedom. The choice is yours. You can't have both.

You have heard of the expression "You can't have your cake and eat it, too!" That means that if you eat your cake or spend your money, then it is gone and you don't have it. Is it better to consume your money on frivolous things a few dollars at a time, or is it better to save it until you have a single large chunk of it to invest into something that will make you even more money without having to work for it? Investing is what rich people teach their kids. Spending is what poor people teach their kids.

I will use the expression — "DELAYED GRATIFICATION" — many times throughout this book. Burn it into your brain and never forget it. All things which are worthwhile take time and effort.

You must learn to think in terms of long range rewards, and not in small indulgences. You do that by using delayed gratification to save chunks of money to invest. Chunks of money are powerful and give you the power of a rich man. Let us use an arbitrary amount of $10,000. There are literally many thousands of businesses that have been started on less than $10,000. If you save just $100 per week, within less than two years you will have the seed money (startup money) to start any number of businesses. One of the businesses I started with my wife was with $17,000 saved over eight years, and it turned into a multimillion dollar business. (I have started businesses with less than $100).

I usually liked to deal in $10,000 chunks because it is a nice round figure, and it is more money than most people have the self-discipline to save. It meant that I always had the cash to take advantage of most opportunities that arose. As you advance, the number gets bigger and then you will actually deal in $100,000 chunks and possibly even in $1,000,000 chunks. You get there by dealing in $10,000 chunks which trains you to be financially disciplined. You will find that after putting the first $10,000 to work in an investment venture, that you will put additional $10,000 chunks into other ventures. That will sound out of reach to you now, but after the first one, you will see just how easy the next one seems. That is exactly how you grow wealth.

Early in my career a man told me that the biggest problem I would someday face is where to put all of the money. I didn't really like the guy very much, or believe him then, but as the money started to accumulate, I could see that he was right. I didn't understand what he meant at the time, but what to do with the money that is wise is actually one of my biggest concerns now. You will have the same problem if you diligently do what is in this book.

Learn to think in large chunks of money.

CHAPTER 15

NEVER STOP TRYING. MOST SUCCESSES FOLLOW MANY FAILED ATTEMPTS.

Suppose you did just as I said in the last chapter and you diligently saved $10,000 by squirreling back just a few dollars at a time. You are terrified because you know how hard it was to exercise the discipline to save that money rather than spend it. Now, exactly what do you do with it? I hope you weren't foolish enough to waste your time while you were saving your $10,000. You should have constantly been looking for opportunities to invest wisely or to start a business with your little nest egg. You should have been investigating businesses. You should have been working out proposed business plans or investment strategies on paper. You should list every detail you can think of including what could go wrong. Crunch the numbers. Ask for more experienced advice from people who know more than you know.

You should constantly be looking for ways to create opportunities. Whenever I drive down the street or go into a store, I observe how all businesses are run, how they treat their customers, how efficient they are, what makes an exceptional employee, ask owners the dynamics of their businesses, inquire about rents, ask about their business problems, and generally look at ways to improve anything I see. I can tell you months in advance when a business will fail and close down simply by watching how it is run.

I can spot a business that is making its owner a fortune, and I can tell you exactly why it is successful. I can also tell when a business is a front company for some illegal activity. With the right questions and careful observation, you can do the same. That goes for small businesses as well as large corporations. There are many large corporations that are on the verge of failure, but to the average consumer, they look healthy and stable. Some examples are K-Mart, Sears, and Radio Shack. Each one showed obvious signs of failure long before the failure or downsizing was announced.

Back to your precious $10,000. You will not be casual with the $10,000 you carefully saved because you already learned the first law of money. You respect it because you earned it. It wasn't just given to you. If it was money you had inherited, or borrowed from someone else, you wouldn't respect that money the same because you didn't earn it yourself. You will be exceedingly careful to consider all of the possibilities before you risk your own money. You now have what is called "skin in the game" so you will think very diligently before you risk your money.

There is only one decision that will insure complete failure at this point and that is to do nothing. Doing nothing because you are frozen with fear is absolutely guaranteeing that you will fail. Life itself is full of risks. You will never get anywhere without taking measured and calculated risks.

YOU WILL MAKE SOME MISTAKES. Get used to it. It is a vital part of life and a vital part of becoming successful. You may actually lose part or even all of your money, but the more you prepare, the more you stack the odds in your favor. You will fail many, many times in your journey to success, but when you make a mistake, you correct what you did wrong, learn from it, and keep trying until the failed attempt becomes a success.

Thomas Edison tried many times to find a substance that he could use for a filament in his light bulb before he found one that worked. He never gave up—ever. He just plodded ahead. He was even known for locking up his technicians in the laboratory and wouldn't let them go home day after day until they succeeded. If success was easy, everybody would do it. Just don't give up, no matter what. Don't give up even if you lose money. Just earn more and try again with more wisdom from the mistake you made. Keep trying after correcting each mistake.

In one form of business venture I lost almost two million dollars. You know that I didn't make those mistakes the second time. Some of my other many failures included a plastic parts business, a rabbit business, forex currency trading, an Indian artifact business, the stock market, a wholesale precious stone cutting business, and a door to door egg business. I learned vital lessons from each failure and I am still learning. Other people have been successful in each of those businesses, but I had overlooked some vital fact in each one that doomed my attempt. I hadn't considered all of the possibilities.

You learn from success, but your failed attempts teach you even more. My wheels were always turning. I kept trying and never gave up.

Fear of failure or fear of embarrassment keeps more people from success than any other trait. Be very thorough, be very careful, but then act. Make mistakes. It is how you learn, but never make the same mistake again. You will do some foolish things that will embarrass you, but simply note what you did wrong, admit it, and go forward. You will become wiser, more thorough, and more successful after each failed attempt.

Remember that it only takes one success to make you rich. So what if you fail nine times and the tenth time you make your million. In the end you still made your million.

Never stop trying. Most successes follow many failed attempts.

CHAPTER 16

DON'T FEAR FAILURE—IT IS THE BEST OF LEARNING EXPERIENCES.

I stressed how valuable failure, and learning from failure, is in the previous chapter.

Nothing teaches a lesson better than failure. Failure isn't fun and we all try to avoid it, but the sting of failure to your ego is never forgotten. That is what gives failure a power that you should harness. Success is valued all the more when you remember the failures that you conquered to get there.

You will never be able to fully appreciate success and keep it in balance if you haven't also experienced failure. How do you know what cold and hot are like if you don't experience them both? If you are always healthy, you can't really understand the plight of someone who is really sick. Life is about experiences. The extremes of life are where you find the buds of wisdom. I really understand how fear and indecision can paralyze you because I have been there. We all fear the unknown. I understand the hopelessness of choosing a path in a wildly diverse and complex world because I didn't have a clue about what I really wanted to do with my life. I was what the motivational expert Zig Ziglar calls a "wandering generality".

What is fatal to your future is to freeze up with indecision. You don't want to fail so you do nothing! It might sound silly, but just pick a field and try it. Read about it and see if it piques your interest. If you don't like it, try something else. If you don't like that, then try something else until you find what it is that you really want to do.

My major career field was from a magazine ad that I read while my wife was filling a prescription at the drug store pharmacy. Something that ordinary can send your life into a completely different direction. The trick is to make a decision, make a commitment, break it down into tiny steps, don't fear failure, learn from your mistakes, keep your wheels turning, and don't give up, ever.

One of my kids fears failure so much that it has paralyzed him. Don't let it happen to you. Learn about what it is that you fear and embrace it.

Sometimes the fear of embarrassment of failure is so devastating to a person who has an inflated ego that they can't move forward. The only solution for that is to shrink your ego and openly admit it when you make a mistake. People actually love it when you admit your mistakes. Everybody makes mistakes. So what. Big deal. That is the only way you will move forward.

For every failure I have had in doing business, I found that my failure was a result of ignoring some basic business principal.

The fear of failure is one of the most debilitating traits you can have.

Risk is a vital part of success. Some failures are an inherent part of risk. To become successful, you will have some failures. The surest way for you to remain a failure or a non-starter is to be afraid to take risks and be afraid of failure.

Don't fear failure—it is the best of learning experience

CHAPTER 17

HANG AROUND SUCCESSFUL PEOPLE AND LISTEN TO THEM. SEEK THEM OUT.

You say—"I don't know any successful people."—If that is true, that is a sure path to failure. If you really don't know any successful people, it is something you absolutely must change. Successful people are all around you. They are easy to identify. They are the ones who are always planning and doing things, reading non-fiction self-improvement books, becoming educated in useful fields, making mistakes and correcting them, and setting short term and long term goals for themselves. They have a sense of purpose, and it is unmistakable by their attitude and enthusiasm. They use delayed gratification in their strategy. They have plans and goals which they are actively working toward. If you don't know any successful people, you are hanging out with the wrong crowd.

Failures are easy to spot. You want to stay away from them. They are toxic. They are the ones that always complain. They don't read books. They like to gossip. They spend a lot of time on social media. They dress and act slovenly. They do drugs and smoke pot. They aren't driven and aren't passionate. They don't have many interests. They don't know much about anything and don't really want to learn. They don't have many accomplishments. They blame everything on others. They go to work in a stupor. They don't have any defined goals. They don't have a fire in their gut and a sparkle in their eye. They LOVE instant gratification. They have a lot of time to waste.

There is a middle ground and that's the quitters. They are the ones that make a half attempt at life and a half-hearted attempt at anything they do. They are a large group. They are full of excuses as to why they aren't moving up. They actually wonder why the world is passing them by. They are always thinking about doing something, but never actually do it. They are the ones that eke out a living but live without any passion or purpose. If you described them as a flavor of ice cream, they would be vanilla. They have nothing remarkable that sets them apart from the crowd. These are the worker bees that just want a paycheck and a 40 hour work week. They don't have the guts to achieve their potential. They have little self-discipline. They usually take the path of least resistance. They think in terms of instant gratification. They are not self-starters.

You have the choice each day to be in any one of these groups. Whichever kind of mentality you chose to hang around determines what influences you each day. Eventually, you will become similar to the people you choose to hang out with. I have acquaintances in all of those categories, but I will not hang out with people who aren't a positive force in the world. Vow to yourself that you will seek out people who are purposeful and accomplished and also vow to shift yourself away from people who don't have positive traits and goals. It is far easier to move forward when you are around others who are also moving forward. That is one of the good reasons for attending college classes and vocational classes, taking seminars, attending lectures, introducing yourself to owners of businesses, and reading useful books.

Hang around successful people and listen to them. Seek them out.

CHAPTER 18

STAY AWAY FROM NAYSAYERS AND LOSERS—THEY WILL DRAG YOU DOWN.

There are some people in every classroom, every place of employment, and every organization that are pessimists and see the world through negative eyes. If you see the glass as half full, they will see it as half empty. It is always good to be aware of the negatives in any situation, but don't let the attitudes of naysayers and losers pervade your thinking so that you see only the negative.

There is another group of people that are simply lazy or jealous of your accomplishments. They really do like you, but don't want you to succeed more than they have because it will show them up. They are tricky because they act like they are trying to do right by you, but they are actually sabotaging you in little ways. They will have a thousand little reasons as to why you "can't" rather than help you figure how you "can". They are not skilled at solving problems, they just see everything as insurmountable. They offer no solutions. After you identify that kind of people, keep your distance from them. They want you to be just like them.

Losers want everybody to fail just like they have, so when they see that you are on a path of action that will make you succeed, they also try to sabotage you, badmouth you, ridicule you, or discredit your efforts. These people are toxic and they like to play mind games. Don't participate in their mind games. Just stay away from them.

Naysayers and losers love to derail anybody bound for success. They operate by thinking the best way to make themselves look good is by making you look bad. Anyone who is truly interested in your success is realistically encouraging to you and offers possible solutions for anything that is in your way.

Stay away from naysayers and losers. They will drag you down.

CHAPTER 19

A PRECISE AND CLEAR GOAL IS ABSOLUTELY CRITICAL FOR SUCCESS. DECIDE WHERE YOU WANT TO GO AND GO THERE.

Just wanting success means absolutely nothing!

Why? It means nothing because it is just a general idea. It amounts to idle hollow talk. General wants and wishes mean that nothing will happen because it covers too broad of an idea. That is too general to act on until it is more specifically defined. Specific equals actionable. When you are specific, you dissect a goal into a precisely definable, actionable steps that makes advancement toward that goal clear and identifiable. It makes the path to the goal easy to follow. Let me explain.

Suppose that you have a burning desire to become your own boss and control your own destiny. This would be an intermediate and long range goal but it is still too broad in scope. At first you don't have a clue as to how to do it because you haven't decided what it is you want to do with your life. You just know you don't want to be a worker bee or a cog in the wheel of a corporation. What is your first step? I am a firm believer in writing things down and comparing things on paper. Writing it commits you to become more organized and clear in your thoughts.

Step 1 — Write a list of your interests. List what you are currently interests are and also some other things you might possibly be interested in.

Step 2 — List them in order of the degree of your interest.

Step 3 — List all of your skills. If you type well, list that as a skill. If you are good at talking to people, list that. If you are good with computers, list that.

The captain of a sports team? List that. If you are skilled with your hands, list that. List anything you are good at.

It is almost a certainty that you will need more training of some kind, but you already will have some skills. If you can't list many skills, it will become obvious to you that you lack training. Decide what training you need and get it. That is a short term goal. That will be your next priority.

Step 4 — Read about each field of interest you listed. Go to the internet and find out all you can about each field, and it will soon become obvious which fields have the most promise for your interests and your skills. You will also want to talk to people in the various fields and ask them thoughtful questions. As you investigate various things, there will be something that will stand out and make you more curious. That will be the first clue that you are developing one or more things that could turn into a business that you will want to pursue.

Step 5 — After becoming knowledgeable about specific businesses, now find out everything you can about the financial details of each business.

Step 6 — Lay out a business plan on paper as to exactly what you will have to do to start your business. It will probably involve working for someone else in that business for a few months to a couple of years. It took me nine years before I was ready to start my most complex business.

That was because of the capital nature and technical nature of the business I chose.

Others businesses I started took only a few days or a few weeks.

Just a couple years is usually adequate.

Now you have an actionable goal.

By breaking things down into smaller steps, each step is easier to grasp and great goals can be achieved. Learn to dissect things down so that the next step just becomes obvious. Be precise. Clearly visualize the next step and do it.

My wise father-in-law, Paul Robinson, was an expert at saying pithy things that cuts out all of the bull crap and goes directly to the heart of the matter. He once said "A man just has to decide where it is that he wants to go and then just go there!" That about sums it up. No bull crap. Just decide it and then do it! If you can't decide on a destination, how will you ever get there? You will never get started. You will be what I once was, a "wandering generality" as Zig Zigler says, aimlessly floating through life without direction and purpose. For God's sake, make a decision and start. Take the first step. Don't think it to death. If you make a mistake, just correct your course and move forward. You will constantly make mistakes and corrections on all goals, so get used to it. I have great respect for a person who has ten different ideas, tries each idea and fails at all of them. Eventually he will succeed because he still won't give up. He will keep trying. I have no respect for someone who never tries because of fear. He will become a habitual failure in life and he will accomplish none of his dreams and aspirations.

A precise and clear goal is absolutely critical goal for success. Decide where you want to go and go there.

CHAPTER 20

PASSIVE INCOME IS THE HOLY
GRAIL IF YOU DESIRE WEALTH

If you desire wealth and the freedom it allows, your prime overall goal must be setting up passive income streams. You will have to generate your seed money from active income. That is your startup money. That means working directly for it for wages. You will be selling your time for money in the beginning. There are only 24 hours in the day, and you will never have more time than that. Selling your time for money puts a limit on your potential earnings. The magic of passive income is that it generates money with you doing little or nothing after you start it. It generates money while you are sleeping, eating, going to school, participating in a hobby, traveling, or hanging with friends. Sounds pretty incredible, doesn't it! It is incredible, and it is the key financial principle to accumulate wealth.

"Grandpa, how do I generate passive income?" I'm glad you asked because I am dying to tell you. It is a result of thinking like a millionaire.

Here is a very short list of examples of passive income and their sources. There are many more that you will learn to recognize on your own as you start thinking like a millionaire.

Write a book. The author gets royalties from each sale automatically and perpetually. The author of the Harry Potter series is showered regularly in royalties and residuals.

Write a song. The writer gets a royalty every time their song is uses in public. Do you remember the Beatles? Their royalties were in the tens of millions.

Invent a product or process. The inventor can sell his invention outright, license it (like Microsoft software), or contract it to another company and collect royalties. The inventor of the delay windshield washer for cars became wealthy.

Start a You Tube channel about any subject and collect fees from associated advertisers and from You Tube. This is a fabulous new pursuit that young people are particularly suited for. Many You Tube channels generate tens of thousands of dollars per month for their creators.

Invent a computer app which you can license or sell.

Buy internet domain names and sell them at a later time. There are some enormous profits in this. A friend of mine did this.

Buy a house or a duplex and rent it out so that the tenant pays your mortgage and expenses. You end up owning the house for free. You might want to study Ron Legrand's methods. I don't fully agree with them all, but he really has some good ideas.

Become an expert at any collectible field (coins, old cars, antiques, art glass, teddy bears, old vinyl records, clocks, vintage clothing, rare mineral specimens), and watch for bargains. Develop a network of contacts. Run buying ads. Develop a reputation for having cash and being a buyer. I have made serious money doing this in particular. It becomes easy to identify when an item can be an instant profit. I love rolling fast money. Keep track of who wants what and find it for them.

Start a consignment business to sell items on the internet (possibly E-Bay). Thousands of people would gladly give a percentage of the sale of their personal items to someone who will photograph the items, list them, and sell them. They either don't want the hassle, or aren't literate enough on the internet to do it. It would become a passive income for you when you hire other people to do it and you take an override and then start another business with your new free time. The fabulous cameras on cellphones and ability to send photos electronically makes this a no brainer. We have a local consignment shop that sells used furniture. It is a real cash cow.

Buy real estate with the potential for higher usage. Develop a keen eye for changing the way it is used presently and visualize what its future possible use could be. An example is converting vacant property or farmland to building sites. Another is to recognize a trash property that can be demolished and converted to a commercial site. Major real estate developers do this all the time. You can do it on a small scale. I have done this repeated times and it is extremely profitable. This is semi-passive.

Make some trendy item and market it on the internet. It becomes passive income when you have other people do the legwork for a percentage of your take. They become employees and you become the boss who makes the bulk of the profit. They can tend the computer screen while you look for collectible bargains or go fishing in Mexico.

Start a consignment shop to sell anything used. People are always looking for a bargain and they love hunting in off-the-wall shops that have unique merchandise. It becomes passive income for you after you get it up and running and hire someone else to run it that just wants a job. Paying them a small percentage insures better performance.

Amazon is one of the best forums for small entrepreneurs to use as a sales platform. Thousands of people of all ages run an importing or manufacturing business out of their garage or bedroom and market through Amazon. The key is to find or make a product that has a wide appeal and can generate mass sales. It is a dream situation for anyone wanting to sell large volumes of items.

Stocks and bonds can be a passive income, but remember that as I stated in Chapter 13, in order to really make any profit you will have to make more than 15% to offset actual (not reported) inflation which I have found to be very difficult to do when investing in stocks and bonds. There once was a time when this worked better, and maybe financial policy will change again in the future to make it more feasible again when they stop printing so much extra money. I have found profits to be much easier to make in other endeavors. I know that all of Wall Street will refute this statement, but those are the guys that are trying to get your money.

An eye awakening story:

I once did a significant piece of business with a guy named John. He was from one of those very wealthy families with national political connections and was privy to some important insider information. John was the kind of guy that could buy a full city block in New York City. He had a favorite expression. John always said he liked "quick nickels rather than slow dollars". What does that mean? It means that the faster you can turn over your money and keep it working, even at a low profit, the more net money you can make.

If you buy an asset for $10, 000 and hold it for two years and sell it for $12,000, you think you made a profit, but you actually made a loss of buying power of your $10,000. Why? Because inflation stole 15% or $1500 of purchasing power for each of the two years you held the asset with your original $10,000. The total inflation is $3,000 of lost buying power like I told you in Chapter 13. You actually had a net loss of $1,000 in buying power from your original $10,000. That is the terrible cost of inflation. A lot of real estate investors forget this in their calculations and the holding costs such as interest, taxes, and inflation of money ruins them. (They actually tend to offset that with leveraged borrowed money, but that is another subject.) If you buy a $10,000 asset and sell it for $11,000 in four months, you only have lost 1/3 of a yearly inflation of 15% which is 5% or $500 because you only held it for four months. You actually made a net profit of $500 which is actually equivalent of making $1500 per year net on your investment. Holding time of any asset is critical. Quick nickels are better than slow dollars. John is right. This might seem confusing at first, but think it through slowly and repeatedly until you get it.

Any asset you invest in has to make more than 15% per year to make a true profit and then you have to pay capital gains taxes on the profit. When you learn to think like this you will begin to understand money.

Use your own imagination. If you find anything really unique, you will have a winner. Chapter 90 on thinking out of the box, and Chapter 91 about changing your assemblage point will clarify more how to come up with original ideas.

Passive income is the Holy Grail if you desire wealth.

CHAPTER 21

RESEARCH CAREFULLY—THEN COMMIT TOTALLY.

Be thorough in your investigations, but after studying everything you can about a goal, then don't be timid. Commit totally, and don't keep second guessing yourself. YOU WILL MAKE SOME MISTAKES, but just make the minor corrections necessary to stay on course and solve the little problems as they arise. Indecision means sure failure, and if you are not fully committed, it is easy to chicken out just before you succeed.

Research carefully—then commit totally.

CHAPTER 22

USE CHUNKS OF MONEY FOR POWER ADVANTAGE. MOST PEOPLE DON'T HAVE THE SELF-DISCIPLINE TO SAVE CHUNKS.

One of the most important lessons that I learned as a young man was that if you have cash in chunks (such as $1,000 or $10,000), you will be able to take advantage of any number of odd and unexpected business deals that arise. Most people have poor financial self-discipline. As a guess, I would say that over 80 percent of all adults couldn't immediately pay $10,000 cash for an item even if the item was immediately re-saleable for $20,000 and they could make a $10,000 profit. They are so accustomed to spending their money for "things" as fast as they earn it, that they never have any money to invest or to deal with. An item bought for $10,000 and immediately re-saleable for $20,000 is a very good short term business investment. Where do you find such deals? Everywhere! Mostly from the people who don't have financial self-discipline. They are always getting into a bind because they spend, and spend, and spend, and then have to sell things dirt cheap when they are in a bind. Undisciplined people are always dumping things when they need quick cash for their next folly. Some rich people also do the same thing if they had never learned good money habits. Most of those are heirs that didn't really earn their money. People with inherited money are particularly undisciplined because they didn't earn it with hard work themselves. I have no respect for that trait. A lot of those people are neurotic because they know how incompetent they really are.

Sometimes great deals are found from successful people who themselves have a great opportunity in front of them, and they need to raise chunks of quick cash. Successful people are always rolling their cash around and keeping it working. Many of my greatest opportunities have come from people who needed to dump land, diamonds, paintings or valuable coins for an opportunity they had in front of them, and they were willing to take a serious loss on the thing they were selling so they could take advantage of a larger opportunity with quick cash. My whole circle of business associates always knew that I kept chunks of money to purchase valuable items. It was a two way street. I gained a financial opportunity by helping them, and they used my chunks of cash to complete their business deals and make even more money. The more successful people you know, the more you will run into these kinds of deals because successful people always have their wheels turning with ideas, and they are always putting creative deals together themselves.

The more you know about many, many different fields, the more opportunities you will recognize as they cross your path. Many of the dealers in these fields have built their businesses out of a childhood interest such as coin collecting or baseball card collecting. I have never seen a poor coin dealer, fine art dealer, fine antique dealer, scrap metals dealer, or antique gun dealer. These people are sharp, and they are always vigilant for opportunities.

The more people you talk to, the more things you will find out about that you can buy advantageously to make profits. I learned about stamps, coins, various collectibles, old master paintings, antique jewelry, artifacts, gemstones, antique weapons, land, vacation houses, structured settlements, and livestock. I have made significant money in all of those fields, and I am always looking for any advantageous offering. Some of the easiest money I have ever made were in those fields. I have friends who have made very serious money in comic books, Disney cell art, baseball cards, mineral specimens, antique guns, cars, airplanes, boats, buying and selling businesses, houses, land, and virtually any and all collectibles, but they have to become experts in the field. A single comic book recently sold at auction for over $440,000.

One of my friends took three brand new Rolls Royce cars in a trade on some timber land in Florida. He was a little short on cash to complete the deal, so he offered me a serious diamond in order to raise the last bit of money to close the deal. I had just invested my ready cash on another deal less than an hour before he walked in my office, so I didn't have the full cash to pay for the diamond he wanted to sell. Instead, I traded him a few thousand ounces of silver bullion bars accompanied by an agreement of a silver bullion dealer to purchase the silver immediately for a predetermined price in cash. I even loaned him a dolly and helped him load the bars of silver into the trunk of the Rolls Royce he already owned that was his personal vehicle. I made several thousand dollars in profit on the diamond, but he made hundreds of thousand dollars on the land deal and the three other Rolls Royces that he traded for. Everybody won.

To prepare for each field, I took courses in each one to educate myself. Gemstone courses, art courses, numismatic courses, real estate investing courses, finance courses, money management courses, stock and commodity courses, forex currency trading courses, artifact courses, etc., etc. I also read profusely and talked freely with experts in each field. Few opportunities would have been realistic for me if I didn't always have chunks of money to invest immediately when the opportunity was in front of me. You have to acquire both money to deal and knowledge to know what to do with it. Either thing without the other doesn't work. For instance, would you recognize the opportunity if someone offered you a copy of the first Superman comic book, a Honus Wagner rookie baseball card, a fine Louis Comfort Tiffany lamp, or a handmade Federalist chest? Would you have the ready cash to buy them at a fraction of their value? The more you learn about many things, the more opportunities you will recognize.

The same goes for money to start businesses. If you have ready cash in chunks, you can simply decide where you want to invest it and do it. At first you won't be confident, but you will get the hang of it quickly. Just make your mistakes and correct them as you go forward. Having chunks of money puts you in the upper 20 percent or so of all people simply by having self-discipline. It gives you power. Your $10,000 is just as powerful as a rich person's $10,000.

Use chunks of money for power advantage. Most people don't have the self-discipline to save chunks.

CHAPTER 23

SEPARATE YOUR WANTS FROM YOUR NEEDS.

Needs are the things you must have. Wants are only what you would like to have.

Most people haven't learned to separate the two. You need to eat, but you don't need to eat fancy foods, convenience foods, nor food prepared in a restaurant. If you are frugal with food and cook your own food, you will free up many hundreds to as much as thousands of dollars per year for investment. Most young people today are really spoiled with food and think they should eat out. Don't do it until you become reasonably wealthy when you can actually afford it. You will save over half of your food bill if you cook at home and only eat out occasionally.

You need transportation, but a $3,000 car will transport you just as well as a new car costing many times that amount. Financing is set up to trap you into buying a car that you really can't afford by making it easier to borrow the money for it than it is for you to use the self-discipline to save the cash and buy a cheap car outright. Buying cars they can't afford can financially entrap more people than anything else in our culture. If you are frugal here you will free up thousands of dollars per year for investment or for vital education in any form.

You need a place to live, but a simple small dwelling serves that purpose just as well as a fancy apartment or house. If you are frugal here, you will free up thousands of dollars per year for investment.

You need some entertainment in your life for balance. It can be either cheap or expensive. Netflix, at a few dollars a month is far cheaper than paying for movies, popcorn, and candy, or live overpriced concerts. Popcorn fixed at home costs a few pennies. Popcorn at the movies costs several dollars and is less healthy.

You know those same people that I talked about in the last chapter? You remember, the ones that spend, spend, spend, as much as they earn. Those same people buy name brand and designer clothes regularly to wear the latest fashion, and then they periodically donate armfuls of those near new clothes to the thrift stores where they are re-sold for a couple of dollars. We regularly find very expensive near new clothes at thrift stores for a couple of dollars and save hundreds or even thousands per year. The expensive leather coat I was wearing in the photograph for my last book was purchased at a thrift store for $20.

What do we do with all of the money we save by spending on needs rather than wants? We invest it into things that multiply our money. If you do enough of that, within just a few years you will be able to pay cash for a Ferrari and a spacious house and REALLY be able to afford it. You will really BE wealthy as opposed to just acting wealthy. The really ironic thing is, though, you will have gained enough wisdom along the way so that those things simply don't hold the fascination for you that society wants you to have, and after you can really afford it, you probably won't even want it anymore. Your satisfaction is in the quiet power that you will have that doesn't need to advertise your successes.

As you are building wealth and success, ask yourself if whatever you are thinking about buying is a need or if it is just a want. If it is just a want rather than an imperative need, don't buy it until you build your fortune enough to really afford it.

Cell phones can be one of your most important tools, or they can be one of your most expensive and time wasting toys and a bottomless pit of diversion. If you use your cell phone to keep up with everything your friends ate for lunch, play video games, post exaggerated life style photos of yourself, or watch silly videos, you are allowing it to rule your life. If you are using it to make appointments, communicate and store intelligent information, reduce running around in a car to find something, or look up critical facts and not just silly trivia, you are using it as a tool. They are called "smart phones" because the way you use them will determine whether it is you or your phone that is smarter. Are you the master of your cell phone or is your cell phone your master? I have seen some young people actually pay more for their cell phone and cell plan than their apartment rent or house payment. That is ridiculous.

Separate your wants from your needs.

CHAPTER 24

LEARN TO SAY "NO" TO YOURSELF.

If you have a life strategy with a general plan and specific goals, you will only be able to stay on track by using the word "NO!" to yourself when outside influences try to divert your focus. Self-discipline is the one thing that clearly defines people who are consistently successful. Advertising, friends, personal likes and weaknesses, laziness, depression, and need for instant gratification are always influencing you to just give in and say "yes" for the moment. While you are building your initial success and wealth, you have to use the word "no". After you have made your first million or so and you have achieved some other goals, you can ease up a little and treat yourself to some of the pleasures you have delayed.

You will either use good judgement and delayed gratification in your young working years, or you will live a much more restricted life in your more mature years.

It really saddens me to see old men in their seventies bagging groceries, and old women in their seventies running a checkout stand in Walmart. Many of them look so bedraggled that they can hardly make it through their shift because they have to stand all day on their feet. In many of those cases, they would be comfortably retired and enjoying life if they had learned to say "no" to themselves when they were younger.

Practice delayed gratification and keep your long term goals in mind.

Learn to say "NO" to yourself.

CHAPTER 25

DON'T BUY NEW CARS UNTIL YOU ARE A MILLIONAIRE.

One of the most common mistakes young people make is to buy a new car before they have already made their first million dollars. Our entire economy is designed to sucker people into buying things they don't need and can't really afford. It is easier for a person to get a car loan for a car that they can't afford than it is to get a loan for a smaller amount that they can afford. I will give you an example from my own life.

My wife and I had moved to Florida with two little kids and I had just started working at an entry level technician position in a factory. I drove an old pickup truck and it was the only transportation we had. One day while I was at work, my truck was stolen from the factory parking lot. It left me completely without transportation in a new town with a family. A co-worker gave me a ride home after work and after I had filed a police report. A kindly new neighbor loaned me his car to return to town the next day to go to the bank and see about getting a replacement car of some kind. After looking around, I found a very used Volkswagen beetle for $500 that would be economical to drive. The problem was that I didn't have any money. We had literally spent all of our money for the move to Florida, so I went to the bank to try to get a loan on a car that I could afford for $500. Remember that it was 1967. The equivalent of that car today would cost about $3000. The bank told me that they wouldn't loan money on a car that old, but that they would be glad to loan me the money to buy a car for over $4000 which was considerably newer, but that I really couldn't afford. That was a real eye opener for me. I realized that the game of the banks was to get people committed to payments that actually turned them into workers for the banks. I had established credit from Montgomery Ward when I bought a welder on credit two years before, so because my payment record was flawless, they surmised that I was dependable.

My next move was to go to a finance company to see if they would make me a smaller loan on a car that I actually could afford for $500. I knew they would probably charge a higher interest rate, but that was my next best choice. I explained my interchange with the bank, and they took my application. They also noted that I was not willing to commit to the bank for a car I couldn't afford. As luck would have it, the police found my old truck the next day (out of gas and with some minor damage) in a vacant lot, so I called the finance company to thank them for their consideration, but that I didn't need the money anymore because the police had found my truck. They told me that they had already processed the loan and that it had been approved because of the clean cut look my wife and I had with two small clean and well-mannered kids in tow. Surprisingly, they even gave me a preferred interest rate because of our financial discipline. We decided to buy the car anyway to establish ourselves in a new area, and we really needed a second vehicle because we lived several miles out of the city. That experience taught me two things:

1) Banks will gladly aid you to be financially irresponsible and loan you too much money if they think you will pay back the money with interest. They don't care how it impacts your personal situation overall as long as you pay them.

2) If you are obviously clean cut and responsible, you can deal with people to your advantage. We drove that Volkswagen for several years, and we did further business with that same finance company at the preferred interest rate.

A car is nothing more than transportation. Unfortunately, in our culture it is a status symbol and an ego extension. It is touted as everything from a chick magnet to a social stepping stone. The interesting thing is that more real millionaires drive old or used cars than drive new ones. Cars are not a financial asset. They are a definite liability that keeps more people from being able to accumulate wealth than any other purchase. You don't need to drive an absolute junker, but stay away from buying a new car until after you become a millionaire. You just need dependable transportation. For the price of a new car, you can start two or three businesses. If you drive an older used car, you can use the money you would have wasted on a depreciating new car to start setting up your passive income streams. I will discuss passive income streams more in CHAPTER 73. New cars typically depreciate thousands of dollars as soon as they are titled and are driven off the lot. Can you really afford to literally throw away thousands of dollars to "feel good"? All of the auto manufacturers spend millions of dollars per year to convince you to make that foolish decision. This is the perfect time to say "no" to yourself and used delayed gratification to your advantage. When you make your first million, then you can actually afford a new car. I still drive ten year old cars, and I could pay cash to buy a new Ferrari or Lamborghini if I choose to be that foolish. My ego doesn't require it, and it is a foolish way to tie up money that could be working to make more money. I get my pleasure instead from investing in great art, rare coins, or rare gemstones which are making passive income.

Don't buy new cars until you are a millionaire.

An interesting side story:

Many years ago, a very wealthy business client of mine bought six new Ferraris and kept them inside in a warehouse for over a decade. By purchasing six of them, he was able to get them at dealer's price. After a decade they were collector's items with very low mileage and perfect condition. He only drove each one a couple of miles each week to keep the oil up in the engines. After 10 years, he sold them all to a dealer for 1.2 million dollars and a very tidy profit. You see, he didn't consume them—he turned them into a passive investment and had fun doing it. After all, who has six Ferraris and makes money owning them? I can just imagine the guy that was watching him drive them around the neighborhood. First a white one, then a red one, then a black one, on and on. Must have been confusing for him. To look at this man you wouldn't think he had a dime to his name. He always wore a torn tee shirt, sloppy Bermuda shorts, sneakers, and had messy hair, but when he spoke, you knew that his sloppy clothes vastly underrated his substance. Never judge a book by its cover even though most of the world does just that. He was one of the most astute business men I have ever met. He was one of my best mentors.

The same guy owned a chain of health clubs, roomfuls of collectibles, and vast real estate holdings worth many millions of dollars. He liked me and offered one of his prime waterfront lots to me for $30,000. He even offered to finance it for me when I was a young man, but at that time I had a wife and 4 kids and a house mortgage. I mistakenly allowed my responsibility to blind me to the potential. That $30,000 was as much as I had paid for my first house. The lot he offered to me for $30,000 sold years later for just under a half million dollars. He was really trying to do me a favor, but even though I suspected that it was a really good deal, I didn't take the opportunity right under my nose and I always regretted it. I learned many things from him, and I always listened carefully to anything he had to say, so in the end I was still a winner even though I had passed up a great opportunity.

Don't buy new cars until you are a millionaire.

CHAPTER 26

IT DOESN'T MATTER WHAT SOMEBODY ELSE HAS.

The only thing that should matter to you is what YOU are doing with your time and money.

What anyone else does, or what anyone else spends their money for is not relevant to you. There is always someone else with nicer clothes, fancier car, loads of free time, inherited and undeserved money, better looks, eating expensive food in restaurants, having the latest electronic gismo or the latest cellphone. Don't fry your brain by racing the rest of the world to poverty by silly social competition. YOUR DAY WILL COME after you have made your first million or two. Spend your time and energy focused on building real sustained wealth.

It is very common to see people who want to look good. Image is everything to them. Their theory is that if they just look good, it will bolster their massive ego, and others will be deceived into thinking they are doing well. They want everybody to look at them and assume they are wealthy because they spend like they are wealthy. They consume their money to look good now, but it sabotages their future. They have to constantly feed their ego, but the ego is an insatiable monster that will consume their real worth by keeping them broke. There is a western expression I learned when I was growing up. It is the description of a person that is all about looking good as "He is all hat and no cattle!" In other words, he dresses with a big tall hat to look important and wealthy, but doesn't have any money to back it up. All of the really wealthy ranchers I have known wear a work hat and own the cattle to back up their image. The big hat and no cattle idiot is just an egotistical four flusher and is a phony with a massive ego. These people are never really successful financially. The only people they are really fooling is themselves. They look utterly foolish to anyone of real substance, and you can spot them a mile away. These same people rarely, if ever, use delayed gratification for long term goals because they don't have the self-discipline for real success. They are too busy just trying to look prosperous to really get anywhere.

The only thing that matters to you if you want to actually become successful is to use your time and money to keep improving yourself and make yourself worth more by continually learning more and by applying it.

Remember that the other guy who is "keeping up with the Joneses" is one of the masses of people who is spending his money to look good and not to actually be financially healthy and wealthy. You don't want to be in his position. Let him massage his ego while you really become successful. He is the fool, not you.

Don't compete with other people. Compete only with yourself.

It doesn't matter what someone else has.

CHAPTER 27

PEOPLE WHO SMOKE OR DRINK OR DO DRUGS SPEND ENOUGH MONEY ON THEIR VICES TO START SEVERAL BUSINESSES.

These vices are very expensive and do untold damage to your health and to your financial future and to your relationships. Cigarettes cost several dollars a pack, alcoholic beverages cost several dollars apiece and drugs are extremely expensive. The downside of being involved with any one of them is so obvious to me that I don't understand how anyone would ever want to get involved with any one of them. They are wasteful and are simply a poor use of your money in addition to how they adversely affect your productivity.

I don't know of anyone in my entire life that was really glad they started smoking cigarettes. One of the biggest businesses out there is selling ways to quit smoking. It also always seemed foolish to me to grow tobacco on some of the most fertile land in the country and then burn up the crop in a product that pollutes the environment, causes uncounted cancer deaths, has caused thousands of house fires, and wastes the productive time and money of the user. Cigarettes killed my mother who died of emphysema at age 57. Her reason to start smoking was to blow smoke back into my Dad's face when he smoked. How ridiculous!

Vaping is the latest wrinkle in how to damage your lungs and waste money. There is a rising number of deaths of young people who vape. Many of them are getting seriously damaged lungs from it. The exact mechanism is still not known, but it appears that the chemicals that produce the vapor coat the lung tissues and irritate them. Vaping was designed as a delivery system for nicotine and other addictive substances. Just another way to get people hooked on something unnecessary and destructive.

I watched my father deteriorate from a vital and ingenious man into an alcoholic over several years. He had the intelligence and skills to become very successful, but he allowed the alcohol to take over his life. He committed suicide at age 49. I don't have any religious beliefs that prevent me from drinking. I just see it as an expensive and stupid thing to do when there are so many other things to do with the money that are more productive.

The scourge of our modern society is drugs. Everybody that uses them to chill out, get high, dull the pains of their emotions, look cool, or fit into the group is actually running from reality. That is exactly the opposite of what successful people do. Successful people face reality and meet it head on. Instead of running from their problems, they reason through them and attack them as a step for a better and better future.

I see one of the biggest problems of our society today is the acceptance of marijuana. It is being touted as a medical control or cure for several conditions, but that is only a minor part of the story. The main underlying reason for legalization is really for the expansion of an extremely profitable industry. It replaces the dis-reputed tobacco industry. It is ultimately backed by corporations and the politicians they control, to sell recreational marijuana for people to get high or chill out. I think the medical side of marijuana is minor compared to the recreational side. The science has shown many times over that certain specific strains of marijuana actually do have some compounds that will help certain medical conditions. The science has also shown that the predominant varieties of marijuana actually grown and sold is for the purpose of getting high, chilling out, or getting a buzz. The varieties of marijuana today which are used for getting high have many times more concentrated THC than the typical marijuana used decades ago. I have studied this in some depth because I have close relatives that started using marijuana as early teens, and they have used it pretty regularly their whole adult lives. The result has been many thousands of dollars wasted on a substance that has severely dulled their drive to achieve great things. They settle for the chilled out mind state they get from running from their problems instead of facing and conquering them.

The legitimate studies with no preconceived agenda conclude that particularly in teen users, marijuana structurally alters the wiring in the brain so that there are certain problem solving and reasoning circuits that are damaged permanently. A spider which is exposed to marijuana smoke can't spin a web. His brain becomes so confused that it looks like a jumble of crossed lines rather than the beautifully symmetrical web they normally spin. The insidious thing is that the people who are damaged by marijuana don't perceive the damage and continue to defend it.

We are heading for a society that achieves less and less because so many people are choosing to chill out and run from reality. They don't have the fortitude to make their real lives better by disciplining themselves to achieve their potential. Many studies and the numerous personal observations of many people conclude that marijuana is a motivation killer and seriously dampens the ability to think critically and logically.

If you smoke marijuana habitually, it is highly unlikely that you will live anything better than a nominal life and never have the fire in your gut to achieve anywhere near your full potential. You will be too busy chilling out rather than getting enthusiastic and fired up to set goals and achieve them. The sad thing is that you won't even know it.

Harder drugs like ecstasy, heroin, crystal meth, and any number of designer drugs screw up your life so bad that you likely will die at a young age anyway, so if you are doing those, don't even bother to read this book.

The financial cost of these vices is terrible. The people who spend so much of their money on these vices are not only spending a significant amount of their earnings on them, but they are literally consuming the seed money they desperately need to start their business, fund their education, or invest in money making ideas and products. It is insidious because the money goes out just a few dollars at a time, but the accumulated total damage and loss is enormous.

I once asked a person dear to me to guestimate a total of all of the money they had spent over the years on marijuana, cigarettes, and booze and write it down. I told them that I guarantee that they would have had enough to start one or more businesses that would have made them wealthy if they hadn't spent it on their vices. I told them to not tell me what the figure is. I asked them to just consider it. I never heard back from them. The farther you go down the wrong road, the more difficult it is to correct the mistake. Also, the more difficult it is to admit the mistake to yourself because it attacks your ego.

People who smoke or drink or do drugs spend enough money on their vices to start several businesses.

CHAPTER 28

MAKE A LIST EVERY MORNING OF THE TEN MOST IMPORTANT THINGS TO DO THAT DAY AND WORK DOWN THAT LIST. THAT SETS PRIORITIES.

One of my biggest heroes is Earl Nightingale. He is responsible for waking me up in my early twenties. He gave me the outline for my life. He was a famous radio announcer with a resonant voice that had a long list of achievements to his credit. Among them, he produced a series of recorded motivational tapes entitled "Lead the Field". I was looking for direction in my life. I had a wife and three kids at that time and was feeling pretty overwhelmed. I was a young manager in a communications cable factory, and my company had flown me to Urbana, Illinois to a management training seminar. The first thing on the agenda at the seminar was to listen to Mr. Nightingale's "Lead the Field" tapes. I strongly encourage you to buy the set of tapes and listen to it. The audio CD version is available from Amazon for $39.95. The CD version is great because you can listen to it while you are driving. It transformed my life. I left the seminar realizing that my management position was only a small step to much bigger and better things. It actually motivated me right out of the corporate world and prompted me to lay out a series of short term and long term goals which became the framework for my entire life. I am eternally grateful to Mr. Nightingale for explaining in simple terms how I could become successful step by step. His words spoke directly to me. His booming voice had gravitas that I still hear in my head even today.

The title of this chapter is one of the statements on his tapes. Writing something down forces you to think through exactly what you want to accomplish. Don't make it complicated. Just using a word or two, simply write down the things you want to accomplish that day and then organize the list in the order of importance. Keep the list on your desk or in your pocket so you can check the list as the day progresses. Work on the most important one and then tackle each successive thing in order. It doesn't matter if you only get one or two things done out of the ten. You had already assigned the most important task first and that is the thing that you had already determined to need the most urgent attention. If you only got that one thing done, it was the most important way for you to spend your time. That is a successful day. Add a few of those days back to back and you will start having habitual successes. Your number two item on the list will probably then become your number one item tomorrow and so on. You will automatically be completing your most important things each day and replacing and reorganizing the rest of the list as priorities change.

I have used this obvious management tool my whole life, and it has been one of the most productive things I have ever done. I physically make my written list whenever I am working. Getting sidetracked is how you lose sight of your goals, and this simple tool keeps you on track each and every day that you use it. The most effective managers and successful people use some form of it.

Make a list every morning of the ten most important things to do that day and work down the list. That sets priorities.

CHAPTER 29

IF YOU DEVOTE ONE HOUR PER DAY TO YOUR CHOSEN CAREER, IN FOUR YEARS YOU WILL BE A LEADER IN THAT FIELD.

This is the statement that Mr. Nightingale made that utterly rocked my perception of reality of what is possible for anyone. The part that resonated with me is that anyone can spare one hour every day to study a chosen field just by using a little bit of discipline. His statement spoke personally to me. Success can be achieved by just doing that one simple thing. Devote one hour a day to your chosen field. So simple and doable, but, oh, so effective. I embarked on that journey and for almost every single day, I researched and then studied my chosen field. Just four years later, I had achieved one of the highest titles in my newly chosen profession, and I really did become a leader in my field. There were less than three hundred people in the United States that held the title that I had achieved at that time.

I have mentioned the following story, but it is so important to me that I will detail it more here. Skip over it if you wish, but this is a slightly more detailed version that indicates my desperation and feeling of being trapped in something I hated. I think a lot of people have been there.

My wife was pregnant with our fourth child, and we had gone into a neighborhood drug store to fill a prescription for her. I hated my job as a supervisor and shift department manager in a factory, and I had just recently heard all of the Earl Nightingale "Lead the Field" tapes, so it was fresh in my mind from a management training seminar given to young managers with potential by the corporation I worked for. While we were waiting for the prescription to be filled, I went over to the magazine rack and casually picked up a Lapidary Journal. It is a publication for gem stone cutters. I had cut some opal as a hobby a couple of years previous, and I found it fascinating, so I just thumbed through the magazine. I came upon an advertisement by the Gemological Institute of America to learn how to grade diamonds and to become a gemologist. I just couldn't get that advertisement out of my mind. I couldn't sleep thinking about that ad, and I lay awake all night thinking about it. The words "become a gemologist" just wouldn't leave me. I conjured up all sorts of mental scenes with me visiting far off places and dealing with wonderful rare gemstones.

I really didn't have a clue where to start, so I wrote off for the brochure from the Gemological Institute, fully expecting it to be of the caliber of the schmaltzy ads in Popular Mechanics about how to get rich sharpening scissors and saws. When I finally got the brochure a few days later by snail mail (this is several years before the internet), I eagerly read through all of the courses offered, getting more and more excited as a whole new world was revealed to me. The brochure was very professional. They described how they actually sent you diamonds and precious stones to study at home and returned to them. That night I couldn't sleep once again because I finally saw a way forward for me to improve my lot in life for myself and for my family by entering a field that looked fascinating with enormous possibilities. When my wife woke up the next morning, I told her about my agony. I told her that I didn't know exactly how, but that I was determined to become a gemologist. She saw my pain and lovingly said "I will support you in whatever you want to do, and we will make it happen somehow." That support meant everything to me because with three kids and a fourth on the way, I was feeling the weight of the responsibility with no clear road forward in an industrial management job that I hated. She always had more faith in me than I had in myself.

A couple days later, I put on my best suit and went around to all of the major jewelers in our city and talked to the managers and owners. I asked them many questions and among them was "What kind of training would a person need to do well in your business?" The universal answer was "We need someone who knows about diamond grading." I was shocked to find out that only a very few people in the business actually knew how to properly grade diamonds. I was shocked to find that most of the owners and managers were just businessmen and salesmen who didn't have any technical gemological training themselves. I started imagining how powerful it would be to start a business, and also, have the proper scientific training and field training. My career decision was born!

We had been involved in real estate as an investment in a small way, and we had a small acreage that we decided to split up and sell. With some maneuvering, we were able to sell a one acre lot for $5,000 and another two acre lot for $12,000 on payment schedules. I wrote up the contracts, and we held the mortgages and financed them for the buyers. I had studied the real estate courses so I already knew how to do the contracts. One of our neighbors who was wealthy offered to buy the $12,000 note for immediate cash at a considerable discount. He offered two registered Angus cows, two registered bulls and $5,000 cash. He had to get rid of his cattle herd because he had sold just sold 200 acres to a developer for over a million dollars, and he liked being able to partly pay me in cattle. The deal transacted because I was flexible and was willing to take cattle and cash. He actually hoped the people would default on the note, and it would give him another access to the lake we lived on for a relative of his. Even selling the note at a discount and accepting the cattle gave us the money to support ourselves for a few months until I completed the Diamond and Diamond Grading Courses.

I started work in the retail jewelry profession at an entry level after six months training. Within one year, I had proven myself as a manager and a salesman, and I was offered the area supervisor position for a medium size corporation. It was a promotion which jumped me over the manager of the Guild high end store I was working in who had been in the business for over forty years. I had already experienced the pitfalls of corporate management, so I thanked them, politely declined the offer with gratitude, and told them that I wanted to pursue a path that would lead to owning my own business. I then went to work for a top end and highly reputable independent jeweler at an entry level. I continued my studies for the next 3 years and completed my gemological training. Eight years after starting at the independent jewelers, I started my own business with $17,000 which I had saved from that job. The first year in our own business, my wife and I made over five times as much net profit as I would have made in salary if I had taken the area supervisor job.

That same year we sold some stones once owned by a European King for hundreds of thousands of dollars. I say "we" because all the while my wife worked in lockstep with me, being a vital part of a team. Her constant support and faith in me kept me on track even in the many times when I doubted myself. My wife later became a gemologist in her own right by achieving the same title I had. She became the only woman for many miles with that title at that time. In our business we divided the labor. My wife was good with the business books and numbers, and I was good with the science and hands-on gemology. We both enjoyed working with the people.

That one business resulted in intercontinental travel, dealing with stones owned by the Kings and Queens of Europe, adventures in the Amazon jungle of Brazil, Peru, and Columbia, dealing in the cutting centers in Bangkok and China, working with miners and dealers from all over the world, working with many very interesting influential and rich people, and dealing with some Arab Sheiks. All of this simply because I heard a set of tapes by Earl Nightingale and acted on it.

If you devote 1 hour per day to your chosen career, in 4 years you will be a leader in that field.

CHAPTER 30

ALWAYS BE PROMPT.

Poor people and also slovenly people are generally sloppy about their time. Nothing infuriates a successful person more than someone who is late or doesn't show up when they say they will. Successful people are purposeful, and their time is valuable. They will literally write you off as a loser if you are not prompt.

One of the wealthiest clients we had was impeccably prompt and respected our time as much as her own. She owned a national sports team, several other businesses and a wide diversity of real estate. If she made an appointment at 10:07 a.m., she was knocking on my door at exactly at 10:07 a.m. Not 10:06 and not 10:08. She had a full schedule and she didn't have time to waste, but she would talk freely and visit casually just as friendly as your next door neighbor. She also rightfully expected anyone she dealt with to be just as prompt. The more important a person is and the more successful they are, the more they value time because it is the one thing we cannot recover when it is passed. Time is valuable. Don't waste anyone else's time by not being on time yourself. Also, don't waste your own time.

I was in the Brazilian jungle on a buying trip. I had set up an appointment with a dealer to view a rare and important newly discovered emerald that was rumored to be found. Unfortunately, I had been in heated negotiation with another dealer on some other stones for several hours. In the heat of the moment I lost track of the time I had made for the appointment with the other dealer, and I was late to the appointment to see the important emerald I wanted to buy so badly. I was just a few minutes late, but the dealer took my tardiness as an insult and literally sold the stone out from under me. That dealer would never do business with me after that because I had shown him that I didn't honor him and respect his time because I was late, despite my apologies. It was a costly lesson, and I never allowed that to happen again.

Being late shows disrespect. Once you have shown disrespect to someone, it is very difficult to regain credence in their eyes. That one mistake cost me over $7,000 in potential lost profit. Just don't be late. I actually believe in the Japanese version of "on time" which means at least 5 minutes early!

Always be prompt.

CHAPTER 31

ALWAYS BE RESPECTFUL AND
NEVER BURN BRIDGES.

It is common to see people in movies or in real life "telling off" their boss or having a mad fit and telling a friend off. DON'T EVER DO IT! It might give you some personal satisfaction, but it will come back to haunt you. You might need that boss's recommendation in the future, and you never want to leave a bad taste in their mouth. Telling someone off only ensures that they will badmouth you from then forward. Never tell off or disrespect a customer or client, no matter how unreasonable they are acting. Just stand your ground, hold your temper and in a cool, calm, and deliberate voice, explain exactly why you are taking the position that you are taking. Even though someone disagrees with you, they will respect the way you handle yourself.

NEVER insist on getting in the last word in a disagreement. You might seemingly win the battle, but you will lose the war. It might seem like it is a boost to your ego, but don't do it. I know that some people are experts at quipping snide remarks to end a conversation. They delight in the "one upsmanship" method of handling situations. They absolutely must have the last word. Learn to avoid this kind of people because they are all about ego. They are petty and trivial. To people of real substance, they come off as immature. Don't take their quips seriously. Keep your mind on your own interests and goals. Always work at problem resolution and don't resort to subterfuge or complaining or by cutting other people down with quippy remarks. Don't use the tactic of cutting other people off at the knees so you will feel taller. Problems are solved by dealing with them step by step. They are not solved by complaining about them. Don't attempt to make yourself feel better by cutting the other person down with a quippy remark.

Another side to this—I have worked with people from many diverse cultures, and I have learned that a "macho" attitude is pervasive in many cultures. If you are dealing with someone outside your own culture, you might be confronted by someone to whom absolutely feels duty bound by their own upbringing to APPEAR to win in any situation. Allow that kind of person a back door in the negotiation to gracefully exit through. They can save face and seemingly win the disagreement, even when they really know, and you really know, that they are conceding the point to you.

I was negotiating on a fine aquamarine in a backwater mining town in Brazil and several dealers were standing around watching the negotiation. We were going at it hot and heavy for almost an hour, but we came to an impasse. Rather than let the deal die, as a last resort and almost as a joke, I pulled out a sterling silver chain worth about $10 and offered it to the cutter. He grabbed it out of my hand and showed it around as if it was worth hundreds of dollars. He accepted the chain as a concession and we finished the deal. I had temporarily forgotten how important it was for a Brazilian to save face. The cutter just needed a way to save face and appear to get the better of the gringo. All of his friends were watching.

This is basic diplomacy 101. It is an important negotiation tactic.

Always be respectful and never burn bridges.

CHAPTER 32

TATTOOS AND BODY PIERCINGS ARE FUN, BUT THEY CAN PERMANENTLY LIMIT MANY OF YOUR OPTIONS, AND YOU WILL OUTGROW THEM.

Almost everyone goes through a rebellious phase in their life. One of the outward signs of it is body piercings and tattoos in addition to drug use, alcohol use and smoking. Tattoos are pretty permanent, and even though they are more popular today than in previous years, they are not welcomed at all in some levels of business and society. The more successful the crowd you are in, the less tattoos and body piercings you will see. Despite the ridiculous political correctness forced on our society, there is still a stigma attached to someone plastered over with tattoos.

Of course, a tattoo doesn't alter the kind of person you are on the inside, but it is a billboard screaming to everyone who sees you that the rebel inside you may not be the safest bet to work with. At least a tattoo that is covered by clothing implies that you might have outgrown your rebel nature, and that you sort of want to leave that part in the past. It might imply that you are probably stable enough to do business with now.

In some of the high end circles of people I have worked with, a tattooed set of arms on a person removes them from consideration from any position of trust. Is that fair? No, it isn't fair, but it is the way it is. One individual defying the world as it is will not make a difference. Don't spend your talents and energy just to make a statement. Instead, use your energy to work on your personal goals.

In my businesses, I could never have had a severely tattooed person presenting expensive diamonds and gemstones to a wealthy socialite or politician. They would never have been taken seriously. To most of society, tattoos and body piercings indicate instability and immaturity, even though they might not indicate that to you while you are young. Very few people get body piercings and tattoos after they are fully matured.

Society has a stigma against different things at different times, and you can either fight it and lose, or get on board and progress forward easier. Don't use your energy to be rebellious. It is a losing battle. I have been somewhat rebellious in some other ways and it has not been fruitful for me. There will always be unfair perceptions in society. Use your energy to propel yourself forward. You are the one who will win in the end. If you must have pictures on your body, go to a Renaissance festival and have an artist paint you for the day. Wear it around for a while and have some temporary fun, wash it off, and then re-join the real world.

Tattoos and body piercings are fun, but they can permanently limit many of your options and you will outgrow them.

CHAPTER 33

POT ROBS YOU OF DRIVE AND INITIATIVE.
DON'T USE IT IN ANY FORM.

I addressed the use of pot (marijuana) in CHAPTER 27, but it is so important that I want to explain more about it.

I watched marijuana kill much of the drive and ambition of three people near to me, and it broke my heart. I sincerely believe that if they had not habitually smoked pot to dull out their problems through getting high that they would be well on their way or would have achieved millionaire status long ago. They were all very intelligent and have a good work ethic. Also, I think that the effects of pot prompted them to make some of the bad choices in their lives that they made. It was very common to do drugs and smoke pot when they were younger. They fell into the common trap of wanting to fit in, be cool, be rebellious, and chill out. I think they viewed straight people as dull, square, and the last thing they wanted to become. They didn't want any part of the "disciplined life" scene. In my opinion, the pot dampened their desire to lay out specific long term plans and diligently work toward them. Several years ago, pot was bad enough, but was weak by today's standards. Selective cultivation, cross breeding, gene splicing, cloning, and sophisticated laboratory testing have been combined to produce pot that is many times more powerful and dangerous than pot was forty years ago. There has been a big push to develop the medicinal form of cannabis which produces a completely different ratio of active chemicals. They have been successful at developing some varieties that have shown to be a serious help in treating some psychological disorders, glaucoma, certain cancers, and is showing promise in current trials to be useful for treating seizures and some other ailments. I have absolutely no problem with that. What I do have a problem with is all other versions of pot that are laden with high percentages of delta9-tetrahydrocannabinol (THC). Particularly, the mega potent varieties available today. It is responsible for the high that users get. That is the pot that the young people are after. They are specifically not after the medicinal variety which has much less THC and a relatively higher percentage of cannabigerol (CBD), and cannabinol (CBN) which are the medicinal chemicals in pot.

The effects on the developing brains of young people from teen years to about age twenty four are alarming. Psychologically, marijuana users train themselves to be dependent on marijuana as an escape mechanism instead of facing and solving problems. This results in training themselves to run from problems and temporarily bury their difficulties by getting high to gloss over the unpleasantness of their lives with a temporary high. It becomes habitual to get high to deal with problems rather than to learn problem solving skills to actually solve their problems which would actually make their lives better. It becomes a repeated consuming cycle. The result is a person without drive and without motivation and without the skills to compete against people who haven't depended on running from their problems. It does nothing less than sabotage their lives and their futures. The longer they use pot, the wider the capability gap and achievement gap become between users and non-users.

The whole notion of medical marijuana is being used to cover the real agenda of most marijuana users. The real reason that most users want it legalized is for the high, not for the medicinal value. Corporations and some politicians are backing legalization because it is an enormously profitable business. The corporations see vast opportunity for profit, and politicians are drooling to tax it heavily like they did to alcohol and cigarettes. Once it becomes systemic, it will be nearly impossible to eradicate, just like alcohol and cigarettes. I personally believe that marijuana is far more damaging to individuals and to society as a whole because it is such a motivation and initiative killer. Marijuana use masks problems so that things seem better, but really aren't. Successful people do not run from their problems or try to mask them. Successful people face problems directly and work on them until they are solved. They develop their problem solving skills and use them because they know that is how you really make things better.

Pot robs you of your drive and initiative. Don't use it in any form.

CHAPTER 34

REAL MILLIONAIRES ARE FRUGAL. IT'S THE WANNABES THAT THROW MONEY AROUND.

Millionaires ALWAYS ask the price of things. They are frugal. What does frugal mean? Frugal is the responsible, sensible, careful, and deliberate use of money as a tool to purchase only the most product and services for the least amount of money. Self-made millionaires all know how much discipline and effort it took to become a millionaire. They are not about to squander their money foolishly. They don't need to make a statement and show off for the rest of the world to see. They have the quiet confidence to know that they have financial control of their lives.

If you see a person throw money around trying to look important, know that they are really acting a fool. They are just trying to look wealthy because they are not wealthy, and they are just massaging their own ego. People who are actually wealthy see through these phony blow hards and are disgusted by them.

I like Ben Franklin's saying in the Poor Richard's Almanac— "A fool and his money are soon parted!" It is so true.

Real millionaires are frugal. It's the wannabes that throw money around.

CHAPTER 35

MONEY IS SIMPLY A TOOL. LEARN ITS RULES & HOW TO USE IT PROPERLY.

Before you can use any tool effectively, you must learn what it will do and what it won't do. Then you must learn the exact techniques that make the tool do what you want it to do. A hammer doesn't work for tightening a screw, but it is perfect for driving a nail. Money is just the same. It is the perfect thing for some purposes, but not for others. It isn't a cure all that many people think. Once you know how to acquire it, then you must know what to do with it once you have it in your hand. Money sitting on the table is useless. It has to be put to work in the proper way in order to be useful. You might say that you would just spend it and that is useful, but what did you get that was important or lasting from spending it that will improve your future or increase your fortune? Of course, you have to spend money on necessities such as food, shelter, and transportation, but beyond the basics, expensive food, expensive shelter, and expensive transportation are a luxury that you cannot afford until you are a millionaire. If you forget those priorities, you will remain poor. Investing rather than spending is the key.

There are many rules of money defined by many different people. In my own experience, these rules are the ones I have found the most useful:

Chunks of money are far more useful than dribbles of money. Chunks of money give you power. Allow small amounts to accumulate into large amounts.

Idle money is lazy and doesn't help you nearly as much as working money. Always keep your money working to make more money, and particularly work to establish passive income streams. All millionaires do this and constantly keep their money working. Cash in a bank for long periods is idle money. Invest money to make more money.

Passive income is the endgame. Ultimately, you want all of your income to flow to you without working for it with labor.

Interest is only effective if you are making more than actual (not officially reported) inflation. That is possible to do but it is extremely difficult. Financial scammers are notorious for promising high interest rates to entice lazy and unsophisticated people who just inherited money, and con them out of it in a Ponzi scheme. This has happened to several of my friends and associates despite my warnings.

Sometimes borrowed money is very useful, but use it with caution and wisdom. Large investments such as a money making real estate and vital purchases will require borrowed money. Read contracts carefully and understand them in detail before you sign. Never sign anything you don't read and understand. Don't be afraid to walk away from a contract written with language you don't like.

Working for a salary or for hourly wages is the most difficult way to become rich. Use hourly wages to establish your seed money to invest or to start businesses and then move on.

It is just as easy to deal in large sums as it is to deal in small sums. A wealthy friend once told me that dealing in small numbers was even more work because people who dealt in small numbers were small thinkers. He said you would make money much easier by dealing in bigger numbers with people who think bigger. He was right. It is true. Small people nickel and dime you on small matters, but bigger thinkers concentrate on the important things. My friend owned a hobby shop among other businesses. He said that he would spend more time selling a fifty cent bottle of modeler's paint to a hobbyist than it would take him to sell $5,000 or $10,000 of model train equipment to an enthusiast who was accustomed to dealing in large sums of money because that kind of customer had his own businesses and could afford his expensive hobby.

Work with people who are accustomed to working with large sums of money. They understand it. You will make more by dealing with them than you will working with people who don't understand the rules of money. They cut to the chase in business deals and don't waste time.

Be studied and careful, but don't be timid with money. Use it with confidence if you really believe in something. If you don't really believe in it, you shouldn't get involved with it. Put your money where your mouth is. Don't spend it. Invest it. Research the venture thoroughly and very carefully, then invest in it if it looks favorable enough!

Very carefully investigate anything before you invest money in it. Always be aware of all the things that could go wrong with any investment, but don't let it paralyze you. Just tend to your investments and react appropriately and timely as conditions change.

Build enough credit so that you can get the best interest rates. Protect your credit because it is your financial reputation. Only use credit wisely, and never create more debt than you can comfortably handle. Banks will loan you far more money than it is wise for you to use. My father-in-law always said that the banks would loan him enough money to ruin him financially, and he was right. I personally worked toward a time when I would never have to borrow any money for anything, and I am there. It feels good. I am the banker in my business dealings now.

Money will have children if it is properly managed. That is, money will make you more money that will make you even more money, and so on. That is what is called "passive income" after your money reaches the stage where it is on autopilot. It keeps on generating wealth without you actually working for it. Remember that working by the hour is only the way to get your seed money. It is a very poor way to get anything more out of life than just struggling to stay even. Some examples of passive income are: writing a book and collecting royalties, inventing a product or process and collecting royalties, investing in a building or land and convert it to a higher value use, start a You Tube channel and get sponsors to advertise, become an expert in any collectible field like coins, antiques, stamps, baseball cards, autographs, and continually watch for bargains which are everywhere (buy low and sell higher), or look for passive investments in someone else's business with you as a silent partner. The list is endless. Just be imaginative and look constantly for opportunities.

Making and holding onto your first $10,000 is actually harder than turning that $10,000 into $100,000. Once you have that, just use the same principle to turn that $100,000 into $1,000,000. All you are doing is just adding more zeros to the number. The initial seed money you need to get started is easy if you stay focused and treat it as your most important mission in life. Treat that initial $10,000 as if it is the key to your entire financial future, because it is. The faster you can accumulate your seed money, the quicker it will start to make passive money for you. By using delayed gratification and saying "no" to your wants temporarily, you will be able to make millionaire status in just a few short years. Then you can indulge yourself within reason. Most people just don't have the self-discipline to do this, and that is why they remain stuck in a J.O.B. (just over broke). It is a self-fulfilling and repeating cycle.

Learn how to leverage money so that a small amount controls a large amount. This is one of the most effective uses of credit. An example would be if you bought a duplex house and lived in one side while you rented out the other side. Say you put $10,000 down on it, and you rented the other side to make your bank payments and expenses. You diligently looked and found a $100,000 property, so the initial down payment of $10,000 now controls $100,000 as long as you make the payments. That is a 10 to 1 financial leverage. Banks won't lend you that amount for $10,000 down, but individuals will owner finance for that amount down. Real estate tends to rise in value in a populous area, so whatever rise the property makes is leveraging your gain by a ratio of 10 to 1. That outpaces inflation by a long shot. All the while you are able to house yourself very cheaply with your renter paying for your whole mortgage or nearly the whole mortgage. Worst case scenario is that they are paying your housing expenses. You can legally take a tax write off for the interest to the bank, take a tax write off on all expenses associated with the property including associated transportation, and build your wealth at a 10 to 1 leveraged ratio. That is just one way to get rich.

If you were smart, and you beat the bushes enough to find a duplex that was really worth much more than you were paying (these deals are out there— you just have to be diligent to find them), you will even be further ahead. I actually have seen banks loan the full purchase price or even more if the extra money was to be used to make the property or its income worth more, and you can show that you are a dependable risk. I always liked to use owner financed deals because I always drew up my own contracts. I liked to deal with individuals much more than dealing with banks. Individuals are far less complicated. Also, individuals will many times approach you when they get into a bind to sell you back your own mortgage at a discount of up to 40% if you will pay them off in a chunk of cash. This is where chunks of cash really can matter. I have been on both sides of that scenario, and it is good business for both parties. The holder of the mortgage gets the immediate cash he needs, and you end up with a fantastic bargain on the property. The owner would probably never have considered selling the property originally for what he ended up selling the discounted mortgage back to you. Conditions change with time. This is why it is important to always have chunks of cash. I have bought mortgages at a discount and have sold mortgages at a discount if I needed quick cash for the next deal. After you get on your feet, this is a really lucrative way to make large chunks of cash quickly.

Understanding taxes is also a rule of money. The tax laws are written by the rich (along with the politicians that they fund) for the rich. I'm not saying that is fair, but that is the way it is. That is why the rich pay very little in taxes. It is the people who work for their living that pay the bulk of the taxes. The more money you make, the more important it is to learn exactly how to minimize your legal tax liabilities. All businesses have enormous tax advantages, and everyone must own at least one business and learn how to use the law to minimize their taxes. Every dollar not paid in taxes is a dollar you can keep and make grow.

Avoid fixed and repetitive expenses like the plague. A repetitive expense can be a weight around your neck forever. Singular expenses are not as dangerous. Compute how much any repetitive fixed expense costs per year. The favorite trick of sales people is to say "It only costs 60 cents a day". That doesn't sound like much, but it is really costing $219 per year. Think in terms of yearly costs. If you smoke a pack of cigarettes per day at $5 per pack, it is costing you $1,825 per year in cash to destroy your health.

Money is a simple tool. Learn its rules and how to use it properly

CHAPTER 36

DECIDE WHAT IT IS YOU WANT AND THEN GO AFTER IT WITH FERVOR.

Half of success is deciding what you want in detail. The other half of success is going after it with fervor.

Another word for fervor is enthusiasm. Accumulating wealth is exciting, and it becomes a fire burning in your gut after you see how it works when you start to have some small initial successes. You will get up every morning with purpose, and you will become so enthusiastic that you can't wait to start the day. Instead of life being a day to day struggle just for survival and paycheck to paycheck to just keep even with your bills, life will be exciting every day. You will start thinking of life as a fascinating game where you are using your discipline, creative reasoning, and skills to make the most of every opportunity. You will learn to see opportunities that you once overlooked. You will have caught the entrepreneur's spirit. Money and other wealth is just a way to keep score. Your creativity for working out deals will consume you and make you a combination businessman and diplomat. You will transfer into "possibility thinking" mode by literally creating new ways to think about things to make seemingly impossible and improbable things happen. Your assemblage point, your point of awareness, will shift into a perception where all things are possible because you now have the tools to make them possible. You are now in control of your destiny.

Decide what it is that you want and then go after it with fervor.

CHAPTER 37

YOU WILL BECOME WHAT YOU THINK ABOUT AND STRIVE TOWARD.

What you spend your time thinking about determines where you will end up. If your mind is filled with inane trivia, fear, feelings of inadequacy, treachery, or any combinations of negative emotions and thoughts, you will fail. If you fill your mind with visions of successful completions of your goals and work for them, you will succeed. Whatever you spend your conscious and subconscious time thinking about is what you will eventually become.

If you have wasted a lot of time in your life by not consciously thinking about what you want to do with your life, your mind will likely be undisciplined. It leads to not knowing what you want to do and not knowing where to go. It leads to thinking in foggy generalities. Is this how you feel?

Becoming successful early in life has a great benefit. You have trained your mind to have many successful years for the rest of your life. The younger you start, the easier it is. Bad habits developed over many years trains you what NOT to do. They are more difficult to break the older you get because they have become so deeply ingrained in your psyche.

Avoid poisoning your mind with negative thoughts. That doesn't mean that you should ignore the negative or unpleasant side of life's challenges, just don't let them consume and control you. Do whatever you can to minimize them and keep moving forward. By moving forward, you will soon move past them and they will be behind you.

You will become what you think about and strive toward.

CHAPTER 38

WORK ON SEVERAL GOALS AT ONE TIME AND PRIORITIZE THEM.

You read in CHAPTER 28 to make a list of the "ten most important things to do". Use the same kind of list to prioritize your ten most important goals. You should have several simultaneous goals to be working on all through your life. This is called "juggling". It gives your life direction and meaning. It also is the quickest and most effective way to attain the most important goals first. Some of your goals might only take a day or two to accomplish, and others might take decades.

Continual reassessment of your list of goals does two things. It keeps you abreast of how you are advancing as you check off the completed ones, and it also makes you quickly aware of changing conditions in life that necessitate amending your goals. Suppose you wanted to get a Bachelor's degree by age 22, but you got really sick or that you had to recover from a bad car accident. It might delay your graduation by a few months. That is still O.K. because you just amend your time schedule to accommodate a changing circumstance. The important thing is that you graduate. You won't always be successful in accomplishing everything exactly on schedule, but you will be right on top of how you need modify your expectations to accomplish the most important things first and keep your attention on what you are trying to accomplish. Suppose you really screw up, and you aren't a millionaire by age 30 as I promise you can be. Wouldn't it be an absolute tragedy if you took until you were 32, or maybe 35? What a disaster!! You would only be a 35 year old millionaire instead of a 30 year old millionaire. Either one sure beats a life of mediocrity.

Keep all of your goals in play and shift priorities as you need to in order to be the most efficient. It sounds complicated, but it isn't

If you screw up and miss becoming a millionaire by age 30, becoming a millionaire at the advanced age of 35 still puts you in the top 0.2% of all people in the world. The important thing is that you are gaining the skills to become a millionaire, and nobody can ever take those skills away from you once you learn them. If you were to lose all of the money you had accumulated, all you have to do is start over again and use the same skills to do it again. Second time around is faster. So, you are a slow learner, so what. The important thing is that you got there. You could look at your glass as half full rather than half empty. You are a success anyway because you got there just a little slower. So what! I certainly wouldn't be disappointed with that. The important thing is that you got there. Consciously working from a list of goals WILL get you there.

Learn how to juggle several goals and tasks and adjust priorities daily for the best overall outcome. The ability to juggle changing situations is an important trait.

Work on several goals at one time and prioritize them.

CHAPTER 39

READ THE BIOGRAPHIES OF SUCCESSFUL PEOPLE AND NOTE THEIR STRUGGLES AND FAILURES BEFORE THEY ATTAINED SUCCESS.

This is one of the best things a person can do to get a true perspective of what is ahead of you if you want to be successful. Read, read, and read some more. Don't waste your time reading junk. Instead, study people's lives. Learn from their mistakes so you don't have to experience the same mistake yourself. Learn from the bold way they created opportunities for themselves by being prepared. There is a very apt saying—SUCCESS IS WHAT HAPPENS WHEN PREPARATION MEETS OPPORTUNITY. Take every opportunity to find out what many different successful people have done, how long their road to success really was, and the pitfalls of not handling success correctly. You will soon find that success is just solving problems. Failure is caused by ignoring or running from problems. You will be shocked at how many failures that successful people have overcome along the way.

In your reading, include some famous musicians, actors, business leaders, religious leaders, politicians, statesmen, and professionals. You Tube has many short biographies that tell enough about a person to be useful. Pay just as much attention to the things they did wrong as the things they did right. You will see that everyone does some incredibly stupid things, but if they do more things right than wrong, they still can come out on top. Everyone makes mistakes. The mistakes are not the sin. The sin is not learning from them. The more you can learn from other people, the less mistakes you make yourself. Learn from others. It is the easiest way.

Read the biographies of successful people and note their struggles and failures before they attained success.

CHAPTER 40

THERE ARE MANY FORMS OF SUCCESS. SOME INCLUDE FINANCIAL, PHYSICAL, SPIRITUAL, FAME, KNOWLEDGE, AND CONTENTMENT.

Exactly what form of success turns you on? Each of us has a different combination of things that we perceive as success. In my case, a degree of financial success was imperative because I always had to work for my money since I was a small kid. Having enough money so that I didn't have to ever worry about going broke, and being financially secure was important to me. As I matured I realized that there are so many other things that are at least as important as financial stability and a person should always include those in their life plans. Knowledge, spiritual enlightenment, and contentment are lifelong goals that will be works in progress on my death bed. I think we should always strive for these things every day of our lives. Health is important, and if you can sort out all of the conflicting health information to arrive at the truth, you are doing better than me. Every day, there is an ongoing battle as to whether eggs are good or bad for you, whether being vegetarian is good or bad, etc.

Fame is something that my ego never needed, and it is something I would actually avoid. If you are low key, you don't have the responsibility of an impossible image to maintain. Others feel differently. They aspire to be famous. I can see its allure, but I see so many famous people who live horrible lives.

What I am saying in this chapter is that "A LETTER TO MY GRANDCHILDREN" emphasizes financial success. It is done only for the purpose of providing freedom of choices that sufficient money affords you to concentrate on other important goals. There is nothing noble or fun about being poor or living from paycheck to paycheck. I know because I have experienced both, and I don't like being poor. Hopefully, you will gain the wisdom of discipline and a frugal nature along the way so that you don't just become another obnoxious jackass with your money. One of the things that shocked me when I traveled to other countries outside the USA is that many Americans are spoiled jackasses and are condescending to people in other cultures who are less fortunate than we are. Nothing is more distasteful to me that people of privilege that think and act like they are better than everyone else with their pseudo aristocratic attitudes. Use the wisdom to use your money and influence tastefully.

There are many forms of success. Some include financial success, spiritual enlightenment, fame, knowledge, and contentment.

CHAPTER 41

CONSCIOUSLY IMPROVE YOURSELF
A LITTLE BIT EVERY DAY.

I know the idea below sounds corny, but it works:

Every morning when you glance at yourself in the mirror, deliberately and consciously ask yourself "What am I going to do TODAY that will make me a better person and move me closer to my goals?" Just this simple five second reminder helps keep you on track. If you actually do some little thing to make yourself a better person each and every day, in a single year, you would have done 365 things that will make you better. These are called baby steps, and it is the way to make a monumental task easily doable. Small steps are easy, so use small steps in everything you do to accomplish big things.

The key to making this technique effective is the word "consciously". If you do something deliberately with your mind engaged, it forces your mind to become more and more disciplined. It forces you into a habit, and then it becomes a way of life— the successful way of life. Most people go through life on autopilot. They drone their way through the day to just get past all the things they are going to experience that are unpleasant. They can hardly wait for Friday. Instead, live your life with purpose and be able to look back on each day with a feeling of accomplishment that you did at least one small thing that made you better.

Consciously improve yourself a little bit every day.

CHAPTER 42

ALWAYS DEMONSTRATE GRATITUDE WHEN APPROPRIATE.

Most young people today don't openly show gratitude when someone does something for them. Good manners have really slipped in our general culture, but good manners are alive and well in the echelons of successful people.

Always respond to anything done for you by cheerfully acknowledging your gratitude immediately and sincerely. It might be a phone call, a text, a letter, a card, or a simple pat on the back with a "thank you", but it must be something. Without some acknowledgement that person will be offended and justifiably think a little less of you. Written gratitude is one of the most obvious traits of a higher caliber individual. Ignoring a good deed signifies a lower caliber individual with poor manners. By responding to the things that others do for you reminds you of just how many things that others do to help you.

Always say thank you on the spot, but then follow that up with some other form of written response if the deed is significant. That is very easy today with cellphones and texts. A written card is warranted if someone expended effort to help you get a job, get into a school, or gave you information that really helped you. A neatly hand written snail mail letter, or even a specific telephone call will let them know you aren't taking them for granted.

I have dealt in all echelons of society and the higher up you go, the more diligent and gracious the demonstration of gratitude is among people. Acknowledgment to people who help you reminds you of how much you really owe to others for their advice, their contacts, their efforts, and their concern for you. NOBODY GETS TO THE TOP BY THEMSELVES! We are all indebted to many other people for the kindnesses they show us. It might just be a courteous clerk in a store, or it might be someone whom you impressed and made a phone call to get you an important interview. It could be a doctor who saved your life.

Always demonstrate gratitude when appropriate

CHAPTER 43

ALWAYS HONOR YOUR WORD.

I entered the gemstone business in my twenties, and one of the first things I learned was that if you ever go back on your word, you are blacklisted forever in the business. The gemstone business is one of the most honor intensive businesses in the world among ethical dealers because tens of thousands of dollars, hundreds of thousands of dollars, and even millions of dollars are exchanged without written contracts. Transactions are made on a dealer's word and a handshake alone. If your word is good, you can literally get a couple of million dollars of gemstones shipped to your office by armored car overnight with nothing more than a telephone call and no collateral. If you ever broke your word, you would be verbally blackballed, and your ability to get shipments would evaporate. You would literally be ruined. You always perform exactly as you agreed, you always communicated promptly with the owner of the gemstones, and you always paid as agreed. I expected the same standard from other dealers when I shipped to them. In over 34 years in business I was never disappointed. The system works because everyone knows how critical honoring your word is. Retribution is swift and catastrophic.

I recall a transaction midway in my career when I was loaned a 26 carat flawless diamond on a handshake to present to a client along with some other very serious stones I was also showing, by a dealer who didn't even know me personally. He did know my reputation. If I had been robbed, or somehow couldn't pay for the stone, the dealer knew that I would have actually sold my house and other assets to pay him. That is the kind of dedication you must have to keep your word. Because I performed according to my word on that stone, the same dealer entrusted me with a deal on a 76 carat diamond priced at over a million dollars. Unfortunately that deal got scuttled for other reasons at the last minute, but I was given the opportunity because of my word to be a part of it. My word was always my bond.

There seems to be a slackening of honoring your word in today's society because slick attorneys, TV dramas, and a lax interpretation of honor have left young people the impression that if some condition arbitrarily changes, you just give some lame excuse and go back on your word. If you are an excuse maker, stop it. Never give your word unless you can honor exactly what you agreed to. No excuses whatever! It is actually assumed that politicians will lie and say anything to get elected. They don't disappoint because that is exactly what they do, they lie. Honorable people and honorable businesses don't work like that. Your word is your reputation. Always make your word good, and the benefits will follow you for a lifetime. If you do not honor your word, that reputation will also follow you for a lifetime.

Always honor your word.

CHAPTER 44

BE DECISIVE! THEN CORRECT YOUR MISTAKES AS YOU MOVE FORWARD.

Indecisiveness and fear of making the wrong decision are two of the biggest obstacles you will have to learn to handle in your life. If you are unable to make a decision, you can never move forward, and you will be stuck in a morass of "what if this happens or what if that happens". Actually, the very worst thing happens if you don't make some decision. NOTHING HAPPENS!! You stay stagnant, but even worse, you lose the forward motion you could be making if you just make a decision. You have lost some irreplaceable time. For God sake, make a decision, even if it is not the very best one. It is a simple matter to correct your course and get on the right track, but you will be up off of your dead butt and already in motion so you can simply steer your resources and energy toward your amended destination.

Indecision and fear of failure has literally kept one of my children from achieving great things. The only person you are competing with is yourself. If you just plod forward and keep putting one foot in front of the other, every time you glance back, you will see that you have gained ground. That is sometimes all the incentive you need to keep going. Just keep plodding forward and you will outpace almost everyone else. Remember the "tortoise and the hare story"?

There is an old saying that in order to beat 90% of the population you just have to show up. Most people won't even show up, let alone be on time. That 90% wouldn't even think to pick up a book like this one. To beat 95% of the population, all you have to do is show up on time with a plan. You picked up this book and you are reading it, so your plan is to become more successful. Then, to beat 99% of the population, all you have to do is to show up on time, with a plan, and then put your plan to work. Congratulations, you see the way to be in the upper 1% of achievers in the world. It is just that simple.

Leaders are decisive. They are deliberate, thoroughly think things through, listen to good advice, and then they make the best decision with the facts that are in front of them. They make corrections as new facts present themselves. They don't overthink it.

Would you follow a leader who was indecisive? Of course not. They come off like they don't have a clue where they are going because they don't. They can't decide. They are paralyzed by fear and doubt. I don't want to follow a person like that. They have never developed decision making skills and problem solving skills. How could they get those skills? Duh!—How about not running from problems. Instead, think things through, make decisions and solve the problems. It's called practice. Keep practicing until you start to trust your newfound judgement and wisdom. If you are doing it right, it will get better every day of your life.

Be decisive! Then correct your mistakes as you move forward.

CHAPTER 45

BE FLEXIBLE TO INEVITABLE CHANGE WHILE ALSO BEING DEDICATED TO BOTH SHORT TERM AND LONG TERM GOALS.

Survivors and achievers are successful because they are flexible to changing circumstances. You must be flexible because change is the only real constant in the world. That fact perplexes a lot of people who want things to stay just as they are because they fear change. Nearly every plan you make will need to be amended before completion. Count on it. Make change a part of each of your plans and goals, but keep your eye on the original goal so that you will ultimately get there, even with the course corrections along the way.

You will have short range goals measured in hours or days, mid-range goals measured in weeks or months, and long range goals measured in years or decades. All of them are important and intertwine to make a life plan. It is an absolute certainty that almost every one of them will be amended somewhat as new conditions arise. Don't fret over changes or try to make things too complicated. Accept change as inevitable and just roll with it by establishing amended realistic expectations of yourself.

I learned that very valuable lesson in my 40's as I was training to be a pilot. I had come to the part of my training where I was flying the airplane solo without an instructor and ready to fly on cross countries. Cross countries are flights of several hundred miles with typically three or more stops and landings on the way. You had to land at specific airports to get your logbook signed by the person in charge of that airport to prove that you made the flight. I went to our training airport with my written flight plan which encompassed three airports scattered over central and south Florida. I had my navigation charts all plotted, my fuel consumption calculations all done, my weather briefing, my wind correction factors calculated, and my enroute weather reports committed to memory. I was prepared and anxious to go. Well, my instructor had other plans. As I was about to go out to fuel up the airplane, he said "Scrap all of those flight plans because you are going to go here, here, and here instead". He had changed everything about my flight plan, including my stopovers, and totally ruined all of my careful preparation. I was really aggravated at him. No, actually I was pissed. I grumbled under my breath and spent the next two hours re-planning the new coordinates, wind corrections, fuel calculations, and different radio frequencies. Looking back on it, I acted like a brat. I thought he was just jerking my chain. It hadn't even dawned on me that he was preparing me for the inevitable change in flight plans that occur all the time for pilots due to weather. That was actually the lesson, even more than the flying itself. I didn't get the point that if you didn't remain flexible to changing conditions, you would stick rigidly to your original plans and would put your life at risk by thinking that you must adhere precisely to your original plan. That was a major wake-up call for me because I then realized that I tended to run my entire life like that, and that I needed to become more flexible to change. Change plans to handle the storms.

Be flexible to inevitable change while also being dedicated to short term and long term goals.

CHAPTER 46

NEVER GO INTO DEBT FOR WANTS. USE DEBT ONLY WHEN ABSOLUTELY NECESSARY FOR BUILDING ASSETS AND WEALTH.

This is one of the most difficult things for people to do in our age of easy consumer credit. The financial system is rigged so that the average consumer is be coaxed into buying many things that we don't need by the Madison Avenue advertisers. The banking system is delirious over the outrageous interest rates they get for the use of their bank credit cards to buy those unnecessary things.

Just five decades ago there was no such thing as credit card debt in America. People saved up their money to make consumer purchases. Debt was primarily used to purchase major items such as a house or a car. The current system prompts consumers to spend everything they have, and also, money they don't have to live for now. If you fall prey to that, you are mortgaging your future and making it impossible to get ahead of your consumption of things that are promised to make you happy for the moment. That is why we are called "consumers". The advertisers use vanity and ego to sell you anything with the promise that the product will make you sexier, younger, slimmer, more in style, more masculine or feminine, feel good, enhance your image, or taste good. They appeal to your vanity and ego because they know that it is the sizzle that sells the steak, not the steak itself. In other words, they lie to you by appealing to your vanity and ego. They punch your immediate gratification button.

I see young men that have spent large sums of money they don't have to buy a fancy truck, a sports car, a big boat rig, or expensive sporting equipment. In their minds, they really look cool driving down the road for all to see, but all I see is a fool that has parted with his money for things that quickly lose value. All I see is an egotistical fool that is a slave to the contrived consumer system.

I see many young women spend ungodly amounts of money using credit cards on fancy clothes, outrageously priced beauty products, footwear, trivial foo foo, beauty shop treatments, and new cars all to enhance their image. In their minds, they really look cool. All I see is someone with their hooks out to snag someone with real substance so they can keep up their selfish habits.

Those same people could have all of that stuff AFTER they really could afford it by using delayed gratification. They should invest all that money and get it working for them instead of consuming it or spending it. Going into debt for all of that kind of stuff simply insures that they will never really be able to afford it. They will live their lives as slaves to the system. They will live paycheck to paycheck and always be on the edge of financial poverty.

Successful people, both men and women, plan long range and invest their time and money on more important things than a false image. They invest in their knowledge because they know that the more knowledge they have, the more they are worth. The more they are worth, the more money they can earn quickly so they can get their seed money. They can start making their real fortunes by investing either in businesses or in passive investments directly. After the passive income starts rolling in, THEN they can spend some on the fun and on some foolish things.

In short, don't use debt and credit cards for things that are not absolutely necessary.

Never go into debt for wants. Use debt only when absolutely necessary for building assets and wealth.

CHAPTER 47

LIVE BELOW YOUR MEANS.

I know it is bad form to use repeated words and lots of exclamation points, but I will anyway.

NEVER—NEVER—NEVER– SPEND ALL OF THE MONEY THAT YOU EARN!!!!!!! MOST AMERICANS HAVE BEEN CONDITIONED TO THINK THAT THEY CAN SPEND ALL THAT THEY EARN. THAT INSURES POVERTY.

Write down every purchase, no matter how small. Keep a simple ledger book and keep careful track of all money coming in and all money going out. This is something my wife and I have done since we were married at 18 years old. We were poor in those days and literally every penny counted. We have never changed that habit. This is the only reliable means of telling yourself exactly what your financial position is at any given time. You might want to do it on your cell phone or computer if you like that, but keep an exact accounting of your money at all times. My wife and I both always knew our financial situation, and we never spent any money unless we both agreed. Our spending never exceeded our income. From our first meager income, we saved chunks of money so that we could slowly accumulate household needs like an ironing board, pots and pans, towels, etc. Our groceries never included any prepared convenience foods. Everything was made from scratch from basic and unpolluted ingredients which are much cheaper than premade dishes and frozen meals. At the same time we were making small payments on a real estate investment. Our first chunk of money went for the down payment on a 3 ½ acre piece of land that we bought from an old man on a contract for deed. We were scared to death. We hoped we were making the right decision. It was! We made a bundle.

We always wanted to look less affluent than we were even after we were secure financially because it nullifies the need to "keep up with the Joneses" and maintain an expensive image. A wealthy boss of mine once said to one of his kids who wanted him to wear an expensive Rolex President wristwatch. (He actually owned several of them as inventory of his business). "I can afford to buy it, but I can't afford the image". If he had worn the watch, it would also require the expensive suits, the expensive car, the country clubs, the expensive social gatherings and parties, and the expensive trappings for his wife and family. He was a multi-millionaire with a healthy business and many investments, but he was wise enough to not be caught in the trappings of the "keep up with the Joneses". His kid was still financially immature and didn't understand what he was saying.

We always told our clients in the gemstone business that we couldn't afford to shop in our own business. That seems silly on the surface, but it really means that even though we owned everything in the business outright, we couldn't afford to keep up the image in our personal lives that our rich clients kept up. Social pressure is literally a heavy weight that will drown you in competitiveness. It is financially fatal to many people. If you don't put on a fancy front, you don't have to maintain the image. That is how a lot of movie stars and rock stars go bankrupt.

WHAT YOU DON'T NEED:

You don't need a new car. Drive one that is a few years old.

You don't need the latest cellphone. Use one that is the model being replaced instead of buying a new one.

You don't need designer clothing. Carefully chosen department store clothing works fine.

You don't need to eat out at restaurants. That is a luxury, not a necessity. Prepare healthier food from scratch. Only eat out on very special occasions.

You don't need the latest electronic gismos.

You don't need X-boxes and video games.

You don't need to pay for I-tune downloads.

You don't need cable TV

WHAT YOU DO NEED:

You do need some form of computer.

You do need a basic cell phone.

You do need dependable basic transportation.

You need basic food.

You need basic shelter.

You need basic clothing

You do need $137 to purchase several motivational books and CD's. (List at the back of this book). It will get you thinking on the correct path.

You do need a growing money fund. Part to be earmarked for emergencies, the rest to be earmarked for investment.

Here is where you will exercise separating your wants from your needs as I mentioned in CHAPTER 23. The world will try to convince you that you need everything and need it right now, but you don't. Instead, you need to put the "wants" in the back burner for now and concentrate on accumulating your knowledge and your seed money so you will know what to do with it when you do have it.

You say "Wow, that doesn't look like how I want to live, being so frugal and all of that. I want to enjoy life! I want to have fun and have nice things NOW!" If you insist on that course of action, I assure you that at age 50, you will still be struggling to just stay even with inflation, and you will never be financially secure. You will be living precariously from paycheck to paycheck, and your future will likely involve menial labor just to live as you age into advanced years. You will be playing catch up your entire life.

If you live below your means all of your life and invest your surplus, you will have financial security, you will actually be able to afford about anything you want, and all of the rest of your life you will have control of your destiny. If you learn the rules of money and always spend less than you make, you will never run out of $100 bills. Which future do you want?

One of my grandkids said to me one time on an outing "Grandpa, you always have a pocketful of $100 bills. How do you do that?" My dear grandson, I am telling you how in this book.

Wealthy people who are wise can stay wealthy because they don't ever spend to the capacity of their income. They have an extremely important quality: STAYING POWER. That is, because they always have reserve money, they are never forced to sell an asset or investment at a low forced sale price. You can do the same by never spending all that you earn and by building up reserves for emergencies.

Live below your means.

CHAPTER 48

UNDERSTAND THE CANCEROUS EFFECT OF INFLATION ON YOUR BUYING POWER.

It is my personal belief that inflation is the most dangerous and underestimated phenomenon in the financial world. I see numerous financial experts gloss over the effects of inflation so that their projections are rosier than the reality.

In my younger years, I studied the Realtors Course books to learn how to draw up all of my own business and real estate contracts. It has served me very well. I have saved many thousands of dollars by being able to produce legally binding contracts that are simply understood in baby talk. Most people are afraid of "legaleze" which is what attorneys like to use to make their contracts seem mysterious and make them seem more important than they are. "Baby talk" is the simplified, but just as legally binding language that everybody can understand. It doesn't scare people when you present offers to them on a "baby talk" contract. In drawing up numerous contracts, it dawned on me that the real estate business is much simpler than realtors and attorneys would like you to believe it is. That tactic of over complication is so important that I have devoted Chapter 97 to it. Inflation is the same way. It is very simple to understand. It is much simpler than the financial wizards want you to believe.

The disastrous and highly illegal financial crisis of 2008 cost us a fortune personally, but because of our conservative investing habits and some diversity, we survived. Unfortunately, nobody went to jail for all of the scams that were perpetrated on the American people.

I mentioned much of the following story in Chapter 13, but it is a critically defining story of our present day financial world and it needs repeating in more detail here.

The following is my opinion as a citizen and a businessman of an event that occurred in 2008.

I watched every single minute of the Senate hearings all through the night. Ben Bernanke, Henry Paulson, and Timothy Geithner testified in front of the U.S. Senators who were investigating the need for the immediate demand of over $800 billion dollars in bailout money to save the banking system in 2008. I couldn't believe how gullible and unsophisticated the majority of the Senators were when these characters presented their contrived and overcomplicated arguments by trying to snow the Senators with doubletalk and baloney. Between them collectively, they condescendingly explained to the Senators that only they alone as experts really understood the financial terms and mechanics of what was happening. In reality, any high school teacher worth his salt understood what was happening. It was a sales job to rob the American people of $800 billion dollars and allow the very people that caused the crisis to escape the disastrous effects of it, and even benefit from it. They were trying to spook the Senators into immediate action and bail out Wall Street banks without thinking it through. The takeaway from the fiasco wasn't just the fact that it was all a scam. That alone was bad enough. The real takeaway was that in Bernanke's testimony, he let it slip that the excess money printed by the Federal Reserve was the usual planned 3%, but that there was an additional 12% extra money printed. That is not counting all of the additional hundreds of billions of extra dollars printed for the later Quantitative Easing programs which all dilutes every dollar's buying power on the planet. That is how insidious inflation is! Every dollar added to the money supply over what is already out there causes more inflation. It can only be accomplished in a phony fiat currency system where the money is not backed by stable hard assets (traditionally gold and silver). Those quantitative easing programs and the bailouts all stole buying power from everyone on the planet that had any U.S. dollars in their pocket or in the bank. It all perpetually made everything you buy more expensive. It also made stock shares look good when they aren't. They are indexed in inflated dollar numbers and give a false sense of gain when there isn't any or the gain is very small.

Realtors have broadly touted that real estate gains of a few percent per year, and that nearly all real estate is a good investment. Real estate can be a fantastic investment if it is carefully purchased at the right price and sold at the right time, but not all real estate is a good investment. Robert Kiyosaki, a famous author, very wealthy businessman, and motivational speaker believes that the house you live in is not an investment at all. He believes it is a liability because of monthly expenses and repairs. What do you think?

Real estate can also be a long term losing investment if it is not also income producing along with increasing in sales price. Actual real current inflation in the USA is about 15%, but is touted by the banksters and the government to be about 3%. They hide the rest in false reports and complicated contrived statistics designed to confuse. In order for a real estate investment to break even, you would have to have an increase in net selling price over net buying price of 15%. That's 15%—compounded per year. That doesn't even take into account the capital gains taxes due on the inflated money you will get when you sell it, nor all of your holding costs such as interest paid on any borrowed money. Fast turnovers of a few weeks are really the best way to beat that syndrome (see Chapter 20). The days of "buy and hold" are not so good any more, unless the property is also income producing like rentals. Conversion to higher usage is also a strategy that still works.

Conventional wisdom of investing also states that buying and long term holding the stock of major companies is a safe bet. The claim is that index funds, mutual funds, the Dow, Standard and Poor, or bond funds provide overall stable places to park your money. Overall, I disagree because of inflation, but also because of the Wild West atmosphere with electronically traded funds that are manipulated with algorithms that buy and also dump huge volumes of market making stock shares in milliseconds. Billionaires and large banks milk the market exactly like a farmer milks his cows a little every day. The average investor doesn't stand a chance against such tactics and sophisticated computer programs. Also, understand that the markets are quoted daily in prices which include all previous accumulated inflation. In reality, the Dow at 24,000 has actually very little greater actual value in buying power than it had at 9000 in 2008. In other words, what appears to be huge profits are really meager profits if any at all. It is just an illusion. Wall Street won't tell you that, and politicians won't tell you that, because the high false numbers makes everything look rosy when it isn't. That is the effect of inflation.

How long can this continue? I have been predicting a financial catastrophe for a long time, and I am not alone. Under their breath, major wise financial investors are quietly preparing for a serious upheaval worldwide. At one time I had significant money in the stock market, but I am completely out of it, and I will stay out of it as long as the banksters and politicians are in charge and keep pumping a false economy.

One ounce of gold in 1920 would buy 400 loaves of high quality bread. Gold price then was $20/ounce.

One ounce of gold in 2020 will still buy 400 loaves of high quality bread. Gold price now is $1,500 per ounce.

An ounce of gold has held its buying power. A dollar has not.

The inflation of the dollar in 100 years means that the buying power of today's dollar is 1.333 cents of a 1920's dollar.

ANY MONEY PRINTED IN EXCESS OF THE EXISTING MONEY SUPPLY CREATES INFLATION BY DILUTING THE BUYING POWER OF MONEY ALREADY IN EXISTENCE.

There are two opposing theories of economics. The United States and most of the world have been suckered into the Keynesian theory of economics where the money supply isn't backed by anything. The money supply is elastic in that the Federal Reserve can print as much money as they need out of thin air without any backing value in order to do whatever they and the government want to spend for. That started for the United States when we went off the gold and silver standard. Since then, inflation has accelerated and destroyed the value of our dollar. In buying power it is only worth pennies in relation to the dollar when we were on the gold standard. Big bankers, big business and the politicians like it because there is literally an endless supply of money to make the phony economy appear like it is healthy and expanding. The millions of people with savings accounts are being robbed daily by the loss of the buying power because the Federal Reserve keeps printing more excess dollars. They call it "inflation" and want you to think that it is a requirement of a stable economy. It is not.

The Austrian theory basically is for a system that backs all the currency with a commodity such as silver or gold so that the money supply is stable. Under this system, nobody, including the government can create free money out of thin air without having the gold or silver to guarantee its value. In other words, not even the government or the bankers can make phony fiat money which has less and less value, thereby insuring that everyone's savings accounts retain all of their buying power. Backed currency makes the banks, big business, and the government fully accountable for their foolish and excessive actions. Those groups don't like it because it controls irresponsible expansionism. Adherents to both sides argue many technicalities which are largely irrelevant to the central issue of the precious metal backed or non-backed money. Like most things that are favorable to specific groups of powerful people, they try to confuse you with a fog of complexities so you will just walk away thinking you are stupid, and only they really understand it. Don't fall for the baloney. One of the best traits you can develop is to be able to focus on the real facts that matter and not be confused by the fluff.

Understand the cancerous effect of inflation on your buying power.

CHAPTER 49

DO SOMETHING YOU LOVE AND FEEL PASSIONATE ABOUT.

The best choice for a pursuit of your seed money might be related to the thing you feel the most passionate about. I was lucky enough to find my lifelong career in the gemstone business in my mid 20's. To me, gemstones were a fascinating, beautiful, a rare commodity, and just as importantly, the fine ones are financial instruments. I was able to travel internationally and meet many fascinating and important people as well as obscure, wonderful, and simple tribal people. The business involved large amounts of money which made it possible to accumulate money easier because you were dealing in bigger numbers. That is a lesson in itself. I woke up every day with the excitement that anything could happen that day. In a few short years, dedication to self-discipline, and a capable soulmate, I (we) were able to accomplish the destination to a million dollars net worth, and we kept on going. The first $10,000 is the hardest. The first million is next hardest. After that, you are on autopilot and use just use the cookie cutter principle. Just keep doing the same thing over and over to produce success after success with a steady easy pressure.

Zig Ziglar, the famous motivational speaker, uses a chrome plated, hand operated well pump to illustrate this point. If you have ever hand pumped water from a well, you know that you first have to pour a little water down the pump to prime the pump, so the handle pressure seals the vacuum in the well pipe cylinder. You then have to pump like crazy for a few seconds until the water is drawn up the pipe to the pump with the vacuum caused by the priming water. After it flows out the spout, you just have to use a steady easy pressure to keep the water flowing. I love his illustration because it shows clearly that you first have to put something in the pump by priming it (your preparation and your seed money), then you have to be attentive and work like hell until the water starts to flow (your investment income), then all you have to do is use steady pressure to continue the water flow (your passive income).

If you love what you do, you don't have to be prompted to do it well. It becomes your identity. It could be music, building construction, writing, printing, auto mechanics, sales, teaching, accounting, medicine, real estate, or literally a thousand other fields. You should have some passion in life that makes your heartbeat race when you think about it. Some fields allow you to accumulate seed money quicker because the numbers are bigger, but even low wage menial jobs will produce enough money for you to save $10,000 in seed money to start a business or start investing-----if you learn and use the rules of self-discipline and live on less than you earn. Maybe the first business you start should be your passion because it will take that kind of passion to make the business a success. I will repeat that. IT WILL TAKE THAT KIND OF PASSION TO MAKE YOUR BUSINESS A SUCCESS. You can't half-ass dedicate yourself to anything. Half-hearted efforts result in failure. Be passionate and go all out. It will make you a success.

At some point you will realize that you don't need any more money, because you are financially stable and secure. You are already able to buy whatever you need, you can buy many things you want, and that you really won't live any better than you do now if you had ten times more money. At that point, what is left for you to attain is any unfulfilled goal that you still have. Life itself becomes smoother and richer because you now have your freedom, and you are no longer a slave to making money.

Find your passion, and the success of your business will be much easier.

Do something you feel passionate about.

CHAPTER 50

LEARN FROM EACH MISTAKE AND DON'T REPEAT IT. THAT BUILDS WISDOM.

I have stated over and over that you will make mistakes. Many of them. If you learn from each one, you will be wiser from each one—IF YOU DON'T REPEAT THE SAME MISTAKE OVER AND OVER. The definition of insanity is doing the same thing over and over and expecting a different result. Learn what works, and repeat it as long as it works. Learn what doesn't work, and don't repeat it. Pretty simple, huh!! The more you learn how to think logically to solve problems, the simpler the core issue of the problems become, and you find the solution staring at you like a neon sign. Just because this is one of the shortest chapters, don't minimize the importance of the message.

You are really seeking wisdom as you try things and gain experience. Wisdom comes from careful observation of what works and what doesn't work. I have one son who is determined to win against a system that he doesn't understand. He has continually made the same mistakes over and over with the same result. He simply will not learn from his mistakes, and he pays the price for his folly every single day. He is extremely intelligent but is not wise. He keeps doing the same thing over and over expecting a different result. There is some disconnect. As soon as you see a course of action that doesn't work, analyze why it doesn't work and correct your action. Ask yourself "What am I doing wrong?" Keep correcting your action until you get it right. Don't be afraid to ask successful people for help. Don't ask failures for help because they are failures. Their thinking is wrong. They can't get it right for themselves. How are they going to be able to help you?

Watch everyone around you, including the people who fail, because if you observe their failures, it will prevent your failure at the same endeavor----if you are vigilant and don't make the mistake they made. Easy lesson! In the investment and business world, their losses will prevent your losses by doing the same thing----- again, if you are vigilant and don't make the same mistake. Easy lesson!

One of the biggest mistakes we ever made was turning down $450,000 cash for two waterfront building lots. We were being greedy and insisted on $500,000. Greed cost us dearly because we ultimately ended up getting only $230,000 (which was a serious loss) when the market deteriorated. We could have sold on an up market and made a very nice profit. Instead, the delay in selling the properties caught us in a downturned market and we lost significant money. We never did that again!

Learn from each mistake and don't repeat it. That builds wisdom.

CHAPTER 51

ALWAYS HAVE A MINDSET FOR
LEARNING. ALWAYS BE A STUDENT.

My wife and I were on a one hundred year old riverboat going down the Amazon River from Iquitos, Peru, along with about twenty teachers. It was very enlightening to watch them. I had been in the jungle several times before, and I knew that the jungle people were fantastically resourceful. They were completely in tune with their environment. The teachers were so full of self-importance that they greeted each other with a pompous "My name is so and so, my master's degree is in such and such, and I also, have a second degree in such and such and such". They were so proud of their formal educations that they referred to themselves as "educators", not teachers. They were so damn full of their educations that they couldn't learn anything. As we traveled down the river and made stops at Indian villages along the way, they saw only poverty, crudeness, and ignorance. Their pride in their degrees made them impervious to new knowledge displayed all around them from people who were masters of their jungle environment. They actually made fun of the food which was simple but delicious, the construction of huts that were perfect for the hot and wet jungle environment and for the bugs (oh, God, the bugs), the fact that the kids could dig their toes into the river mud for traction to scurry up the steep slippery Amazon banks while the "educators" slipped and slid around in their tennis shoes. They even made fun of the way the native people dressed as they themselves dripped sweat down their own faces from wearing too many clothes. I couldn't believe that educated people could be so closed minded. I never stopped asking questions of the natives and the guides, but not a one of the "educators" asked a single question! They acted like they knew it all. I came away from the trip expanding my understanding of their survival techniques, their jungle medicines, their methods of hunting and fishing, and their reason for the way they constructed their huts the way they did. The "educators" came away from the trip learning very little, but with their pride and pomposity intact. What a lesson in how ego can keep you from learning.

Ask questions constantly, and keep asking them until you get answers that tell you what you want to know. Present yourself as a student in conversations. Don't act and think that you need to show how much you know. Forget your ego and your image. The "educators" I described above couldn't learn much because they were too interested in their image of already knowing it all. Be open and willing to learn in ALL circumstances. You can quietly decide later whether the information you are being given is valid or not. Never pass up an opportunity to learn from a successful person. Never pass up an opportunity to just shut up and listen. They are the ones who are generally willing to share valuable information to anyone they perceive as serious.

I always ask many more questions in conversations than the other person does. It is not to be nosy, it is because everyone wants to talk about themselves if you let them. People will openly tell you many important things that will help you understand and appreciate them. You will walk away from the conversation a bit smarter, but since they didn't ask questions, they didn't learn nearly as much. Asking questions is one of the best conversation starters.

Always have a mindset for learning. Always be a student.

CHAPTER 52

ADMIT YOUR MISTAKES QUICKLY AND OPENLY. IT BREEDS CONFIDENCE.

Would you rather follow someone who never admitted to a mistake or would you rather follow someone who admitted their mistake quickly, corrected course, and was open about it?

I have watched many company heads, a litany of politicians and also, have known some people personally who absolutely would never admit to a mistake. Let alone say "I'm sorry!" They seem to think that admitting a mistake shows weakness or they are simply too proud and full of ego to admit when they are wrong. I have no respect for that trait.

I have confidence in anyone who tries things and learns from their experiences. Even more importantly, I have more confidence if someone is willing to admit to themselves and to the world that they are fallible and not perfect when they openly admit a mistake. I want to deal with real people, not people that have to maintain an inflated image at all costs. Admitting mistakes is good for the soul. When I see someone hide a mistake, it makes me wary of all the other hidden secrets they have that I need to guard against. That trait has served me very well in sizing up people in business deals, and helps to tell me who can be trusted and who can't.

I had an uncle who was a full bird Colonel in the Army and was in charge of the food inspection of all military bases for the western half of the United States. When I was 15 years old, he was describing someone who was passed over for promotion. He said, "Pride and ego are worth nothing to you in life." I have thought about that many times since then, and he is right. Prideful people are always trying to maintain their perceived superiority.

Ego keeps you from admitting mistakes and learning from them. How will other people know that you learned from your mistake unless you admit it to yourself and to them?

Admit your mistakes quickly and openly. It breeds confidence.

CHAPTER 53

EVERYBODY CAN DO SOMETHING BETTER THAN YOU. WATCH AND LEARN.

It is easy to underestimate other people. I am constantly surprised and pleased to see anyone do something that is skillful and extraordinary that I hadn't expected. Every person on the planet has a unique set of experiences and skills that is different from your own. That simply means that while you were doing something else, they were also learning something you don't know about. For instance, while you attended college, someone else might have gone to work in some profession such as electrical contractor's work. You might be able to understand math equations and write skillfully, but that other person knows how to correctly and safely wire your house, and you don't. I am amazed by artists who can create a mood and a form of perceived reality by painting a three dimensional looking representation of reality on a two dimensional surface. They understand things about light and perception that I never will.

Recognize that all of those unique experiences which each of us have, make everyone able to teach us something. If you are wise, you will always be open to anything you can learn from anyone. Sometimes what you learn can even be something negative, that is, something you learn not to do. Anything you can learn from someone else's mistake prevents you from making the same mistake.

It is a serious mistake to look down on other people, even if they are ignorant to the skills of success which I hope you are starting to understand. Even losers have something to teach each of us. Find out what it is, and as you walk away from that person, you will have become better because of them. To reciprocate, try to leave something with them that will also help them.

Everyone can do something better than you. Watch, listen, and learn.

CHAPTER 54

EACH DAY, REVIEW THE MISTAKES YOU MADE YESTERDAY.

This is one of the most effective techniques my wife and I used in our businesses. Each day we would briefly discuss any mistakes we had made the day before. Sometimes it was an unwise purchase, sometimes it was a better way to handle a difficult client, sometimes it was a way to work more efficiently.

You don't have to dwell on mistakes, just review briefly the things you did wrong during the heat of the battle the day before. Figure out exactly what you want to do to correct it, and then just do it better the next time. By reviewing how you handled something, you build the habit of handling situations with a cool head the next time. You build the habit of critical thinking on a moment by moment basis, and it helps you avoid making a chain of more serious mistakes.

Part of pilot training is to interrupt a chain of decisions that lead to disasters like a plane crash. The National Transportation and Safety Board has done exhaustive studies on this phenomenon, and they have concluded that almost all plane crashes are caused from a series of several smaller individual actions that lead to greater and greater consequences. If any one of the smaller decisions was altered, the chain of events would be broken, and the accident wouldn't happen. By reviewing mistakes daily, you break the chain of events which would lead to longer term difficulties, and you become more effective.

Each day, review the mistakes you made yesterday.

CHAPTER 55

DON'T LOAN MONEY TO FRIENDS AND RELATIVES.

This might seem like a harsh thing to say at first glance, but in reality it is the best way to keep your friends and relatives on a friendly basis. Why is it that they need to borrow money from you? Is it that they aren't using good judgment with their own money? That is usually the case. Your journey to success will require all of your resources to be focused on your own efforts. They are responsible for their own lives. Usually, people who are continually wanting to borrow money are actually leeches that always have a hard luck tale, a sad situation, or an emergency. Why didn't they plan for problems and emergencies like I suggest for you to do?

There were many times in my life when I was approached by both friends and relatives who didn't manage their own money, but they expected me to come to their rescue and save them from their own folly. YOU CAN'T HELP SOMEONE WHO WON'T HELP THEMSELVES. They are destined for a marginal and failed life, and they are the very last people who will listen to good advice. They are usually in the desperate position they are in to need money because they have already ignored good council their whole lives. They probably have a welfare mentality, and expect anybody but themselves to solve their problems for them. They are the same people who actually believe that if they just had some money all of their problems would be solved. How foolish! Financial problems are only solved when you know how to make and hold onto money and make it grow. Simply having some money doesn't solve anything. Don't become an enabler. Develop the judgment to know when you need to step up and help someone without diminishing their own initiative. Then, only help people who WILL help themselves. The others deserve their fate.

I have watched several friends try to be the nice guy and loan money to friends and relatives, only to have the person stiff them and not pay the money back. It always caused hard feelings and usually ended with the friendship being severely strained for years to come. Often they never get their money back.

It has been said that if the money was distributed evenly among all people in the world so that everyone had the same amount, within a year the money would find its way back to most of the people who had it in the first place because they are the ones who have the skills to make it. The others would be broke again because of their habits. What do you think?

Don't loan money to friends and relatives.

CHAPTER 56

CARRY YOURSELF TO LOOK SUCCESSFUL AND ACT SUCCESSFUL.

Successful people have a confident look which says to the rest of the world that they know where they are going, and they know how to get there. It is not boastful nor is it conceited and uppity. It simply is an outward expression of an inward conviction. I have heard it described as "command presence". It is the look of a leader.

Think of yourself as successful because as you read this book, without even recognizing it, you are on your way to getting there. The first step toward accomplishing a goal is realizing that it exists. By reading this book, you have already done that. Hold your shoulders back, walk with confidence and dignity, be pleasant, don't talk nonsense, ask serious questions, always remain curious, and remain alert. How would you react to someone who displayed those traits?

Carry yourself to look successful and act successful.

CHAPTER 57

CHOOSE FRIENDS WHO ARE CONSTANTLY IMPROVING THEMSELVES.

I already briefly mentioned this, but it is very important. You will become very similar to the people you hang out with. Your intellectual level of thought, your aspirations, your opinions, your energy level, and single mindedness will all be averaged out as a combination of you and your closest friends. If you hang out with motivated and goal oriented people, you will boost your own position with their enthusiasm and energy. It will rub off onto you, and you will become better yourself. If you hang out with complainers, and people who don't have defined plans they are actively working on, you will fall into the cycle of complaining about the world rather than changing your situation for the better. You will tend to think more like them and act more like them the longer you are around them. Drop any friends who have no worthy goals or friends that say they have goals, but aren't doing anything to achieve them. Talk is cheap. People who talk without action are just wishers. In five years they will still be pretty much where they are today. They will still be complaining about everything around them just as they were five years ago. Don't waste your time and energy on losers. Also, don't feel sorry for them because they are deciding their own fate.

Choose friends who are constantly improving themselves.

CHAPTER 58

SUCCESSFUL PEOPLE HAVE LEARNED SUCCESSFUL HABITS.

What are successful habits? They are all over the pages of this book. They are any habit that helps you achieve worthy goals. The list is very extensive, but they include everything on the following list and many more:

Set a series of worthy goals and work toward them.

Listen to other successful people.

Analyze what you hear.

Read books by motivational experts.

Read biographies of successful people in many fields.

Always live below your income.

Save money to accumulate seed money and invest it.

Be polite.

Be prompt.

Tell the truth and honor your word

After a hard day's work, MAKE the time to do something for your future.

Think out of the box and be creative.

Avoid people who mentally, psychologically, or physically drag you down.

Avoid gossipers and complainers.

Watch motivational blogs on You Tube.

Constantly correct and improve yourself by being introspective.

Trust your own judgment more as you learn more.

Take responsibility for all of your actions.

Cultivate self-discipline and delayed gratification.

Learn from your own mistakes and other people's mistakes.

That list is just twenty things. Those twenty things alone will make you successful if you follow them. Any one of them will improve your life. This book describes many more, and you will be able to add your own items with each success you achieve. To develop a habit, all you have to do is to do the same thing over, and over and over until it becomes second nature and is automatic.

Successful people teach their children respect for all kinds of knowledge, and to recognize when they need to consult others with specific knowledge and use it.

Successful people have learned to develop successful habits.

CHAPTER 59

STUDY POOR PEOPLE AND DETERMINE WHY THEY WILL ALWAYS BE POOR.

Poor people have poor habits. They continue to remain poor because of those habits. They are not poor due to outside circumstances.

If you are born into poverty, it is a disadvantage, but you don't have to stay there. The wonderful thing about America is that anyone can climb out of poverty if they use their mind to develop the right thinking skills and attitudes to use them. They simply have to start doing more and more of the twenty things listed in CHAPTER 58 or even better yet, do more of the one hundred things covered in this entire book. They don't have to be particularly smart. Actually, some of the smartest people I know are the least successful because they never learned successful life skills. They just relied on their intellect. Intellect alone doesn't cut it. Hating to be poor is one of the highest motivators. It was for me, because I didn't like anything about being poor or just living from paycheck to paycheck. I was absolutely determined to do something about it one step at a time over several years. Being poor was so degrading and unpleasant for me that I vowed to climb out of that kind of struggling existence and never be poor again. I knew that I was intelligent, but I hadn't learned the skills of success yet. It was so important to me to overcome poverty that I really didn't need any other motivational encouragement. If you want to accomplish something badly enough, you will find a way, and I did. This book is paving the path for you to do the same thing, if you have the intelligence to learn the lessons and the resolve to apply them.

You will see many more poor people buying lottery tickets than rich people.

You will see many more poor people buying at convenience stores than rich people. Convenience store prices are high.

You will see many more poor people requiring instant gratification than rich people.

You will see many more poor people wasting their time than rich people.

You will see many more poor people spending money on tattoos than rich people.

You will see many more poor people who don't read books than rich people.

You will see many more poor people abusing credit cards than rich people.

You will see many more poor people spending past their income than rich people.

You will see many more poor people dribbling out their cash on stupid things than rich people.

You will see many more poor people with no direction in life than rich people.

You will see many more poor people with substance abuse problems than rich people.

You will see many more poor people who don't listen to good advice than rich people.

You will see many more poor people with anger management issues than rich people.

You will see many more poor people who blame others for their lack of money and lack of success than rich people.

The list goes on and on. These bad habits and many more go into the mindset of poor people that keep them poor. All they would have to do to climb out of poverty is change their thinking, learn successful skills, and accept responsibility for their position in the world. It's not their fault if they were born poor, but it is their fault for not climbing out of poverty. To climb out of poverty, poor people must learn and apply enough traits of successful people to change their circumstances. It is easy to blame the government, the world, the economy, the social system, their skin color, or bad luck for personal failure. The real culprit is the mind-set of the person staring back at them from the mirror. Excuses are easy, and changing requires work. Poor people have an excuse for everything. They are experts at making up reasons for their continued failure.

Analyze each person you see that just can't make things work, and figure out what it is in their personality that keeps them down. It will be the things I discuss in this book. When you can see the deficiencies in others, turn that observation back onto yourself, and you will also see the reason for your own failures.

A person will remain poor until they want to be rich more than they want to be complacent and remain poor.

The famous financial and motivational guru, Robert Kiyosaki, states in one of his videos that poor people will remain poor because they are lazy and unwilling to acquire the knowledge that will help them. He believes that you can't help somebody who won't help themselves. I strongly agree. Are you willing to do the work to help yourself or would you rather just complain about being poor?

Poor people, middle class people, and unsuccessful people teach their children to become cogs in a wheel and to fear authority. They live their lives in fear to various degrees, and it keeps them from aspiring to become better.

Study poor people and determine why they will always be poor.

CHAPTER 60

FOCUS YOUR ENERGY WITH LASER PRECISION, BUT BE AWARE AROUND YOU.

At one time in my career, I had the opportunity to purchase the small, two story office building where I was renting office space. The price was $1.2 million. I could likely have negotiated the price down to $1.1 million dollars or maybe even down to $1 million. I thought long and hard about the wisdom of doing it. If I bought it, the appreciation of the real estate was very enticing, and the fact that it would eliminate our rental space cost was also a plus. My reservation was that I was already in a business that required significant technical expertise, large capital outlay, and a very large time commitment. I was afraid that divided attention and capital would hurt my main professional business because I would be less focused from worrying about leases, tenant complaints, building maintenance, and legal issues. Knowing my own temperament, I decided against buying it. I chose to focus on my primary business for several years. There would be plenty of time later to do more real estate. I had remembered the saying by Andrew Carnegie. "Put all your eggs in one basket and then watch that basket!" I chose to do just that, and I have never been sorry, even though I do believe that I would have made significant money on the building. My mind and attention was free to concentrate on important clients so that my commitment to them didn't suffer. Sometimes it is far better to focus on one thing, but at the same time be aware of the bigger picture. It is a constant juggling act.

Focus wholeheartedly on each goal until it is fully under control, and then expand or diversify your time and assets to include the next goal into the picture. Diversifying is critical, but it must be done at the right time or it will destroy your focus before the goal is fully reached. For instance, if your primary goal is a college education, focus on that, and do it wholeheartedly before you expand into other pursuits. When you have your degree, then do other things and do them wholeheartedly with laser focus.

If your focus is real estate, get income streams established before diversifying.

If your focus is on a business, get it on a good profit footing and stable before starting a second pursuit too soon.

When you find the thing that works the best, keep your focus on that pursuit.

In other words, don't get too many irons in the fire so that it blurs your attention and you businesses suffer.

Focus your energy with laser precision, but be aware around you.

CHAPTER 61

MONEY ALONE DOESN'T BUY HAPPINESS BUT IT SURE HELPS.

Money buys you freedom from drudgery, but it doesn't buy happiness in and of itself. Money can be used for good or can be used foolishly. Money brings a new responsibility to you to be a good steward. Right now one of my biggest concerns is how to pass on some money to my family without them self-destructing. The ones that understand money already, can absorb more money and handle it responsibly, but they already have accumulated their own. The ones who don't already understand money don't have it. They would be destroyed by it because they don't understand it. The ones that don't understand it presently are ignorant of their folly. They are the ones who won't listen. They don't know how much that they don't know. Sounds kind of like a Zen Buddhist koan.

Most people think that having money to just buy more things is the answer. They think that being able to spend wildly will make them happy. It won't! Until spending money is actually distasteful to you, you don't understand money. Money is simply a tool and means nothing in and of itself. Not being poor is a wonderful thing as long as you maintain your perspective. If you learn the skills in this book, you can regenerate your fortune over and over and never remain poor even if you were to lose everything. The interesting thing is that if you learn the skills in this book, you will never have to regenerate your fortune because you will never lose it, but you could if you had to. That, my friend, is as financially secure as you can ever be.

Happiness is a lot easier to attain and keep if you have money than it is without money. Without money, life takes on a struggling survival mode. With money, life is an open opportunity to fill with accomplishments and good experiences if you use the money wisely.

Money easily corrupts many people. Can you handle it responsibly without self-destructing?

If you are one of my grandkids, call me and tell me exactly how you will do that.

I recently read that Arnold Schwarzenegger once said that he wasn't any happier with $50 million than he was with $48 million. I like his perspective. I think money was important to him, but that he had a grasp of its limitations at the same time.

Money alone doesn't buy happiness, but it sure helps.

CHAPTER 62

THE WRONG MATE WILL DESTROY YOU.

I was really lucky, but was also cognizant at a very young age that the right mate will multiply your life in ways you can't even imagine. I also knew that the wrong mate will destroy you. I found the right mate and recognized it very young. We both recognized the important traits that would make a strong lifelong bond, and we married at 18 years old. Most young people are enamored with sexual attraction, good looks, a toned body, fun behavior, "cool" attitudes, quippy conversation, and stylish clothes. We both looked beyond all of that. There is nothing wrong with any of that, BUT, the really important things are:

Religious compatibility

Mutual respect

Politics

Work ethic

Money and finances

Spending habits

Ability to set and achieve long term plans and goals

Education—both present and future educational goals

Compatibility of individual and combined goals

Ability to delay gratification for long term goals

Intelligence—both IQ and common sense

Child rearing and discipline

Sex—frequency, level of importance, and type

Birth control and number of children

Motivation and aspirations

Ethics and honesty

Willingness to communicate—always

Putting your mate before yourself—always

The aching feeling that you couldn't exist without your mate

Physical and intellectual attraction

Intense conversation for hours without boredom

Purity of motives

Reaction and ability to function well under pressure

Good problem solving skills

If you have not already discussed each and every single one of these topics at great lengths with your potential mate, you are not even close to being ready for marriage.

The common thing today is to start a relationship with sexual attraction and avoid the important issues. The really important issues keep getting pushed to the back burner because one or both people in a couple are afraid to interrupt the sex with possible disagreements over the important issues, so the issues get buried. The important issues never get discussed. The couple gets married, and it sets the stage for impasses over time that lead to divorce. It is an absolute certainty, and you are kidding yourself if you think otherwise. Don't get me wrong, sex is extremely important in a marriage, but sex is no more important than any of the other issues on that list. Orgasms are really fun, but they don't make up for incompatibility in other things that are vital to physical, mental, emotional, and psychological health in a good marriage.

The right mate will bring out the very best in you by correcting you when you act badly. They will tell you when you are wrong. The right mate will have the courage and sense of self to stand up to you when you are wrong. It is up to you to listen to them and trust their judgment as well as your own. If you can't do that, you have no business marrying them. The right mate will stand up for what they know is right. We are all wrong sometimes, and we all need that exterior force to call us out when we are wrong. The right mate will kick you in the butt whenever it is warranted without hesitation. The wrong mate will allow you to get away with poor behavior. The right mate is the centering influence in your life, and you are the same for them. The honor and respect must go both ways equally.

The right mate will bring out the very best in you and make you the best version of yourself. Examples of that are encouraging further education and training for you both, mutually planned goals, careful financial planning, and insistence on responsible behavior.

The wrong mate will allow you to indulge your weaknesses and vices so that you will slide into a diminished version of yourself. Examples of that are doing drugs together, being slovenly or lazy, and aimlessly wasting time without any defined goals or direction, or spending money irresponsibly.

If your mate never corrects you, they are definitely the wrong person to marry.

Unhealthy and doomed relationships are selfish and dishonest. In those relationships, one of the partners always submits to the other. They are contentious and one sided. Both partners don't stand tall and voice their views to insist on responsible behavior. Over time they end up as abusive relationships and end in disaster.

In strong and loving relationships, one person and their mate are not just a sum of two. The power of two people working in lockstep is more like the power of four individual people, because the unity of two people pulling together in lockstep is not dissipated with different end goals. Two people pulling in different directions never works because they cancel each other out.

The wrong mate will destroy you.

CHAPTER 63

THE WRONG FRIENDS WILL
HOGTIE YOUR AMBITIONS.

People like to be accepted as one of the group. They want a hint of individuality, but most people also want to be pretty much like everyone else around them. They really don't want anyone in the group to excel more than just a little bit. They get jealous and resentful if one of the group works harder and accomplishes a lot more than they have accomplished themselves. It is human nature.

The exception to that is the people who are going full speed ahead with their own plans and goals. That type of person wants to be around others that see a brighter future because it is what they believe in themselves. Those are the people who are headed for financial stability and a higher level of achievement in all aspects of their lives. They will stand out from the crowd.

People like to live at a level of comfort and familiarity. It is easy. Stretching a little bit beyond your comfort level is a trait of achievers, and is a trait that is important to develop. If you just want to be one of the pack, you are wasting your time reading this book. If you want to make your tomorrows better than today and better than yesterday, you will have to distinguish yourself from the pack by being ambitious. Move away from anyone who does not share your sense of ambition to better yourself. This advice includes girlfriends and boyfriends. Non ambitious people will psychologically hold you down because your achievements will remind them of their laziness and failures. If you continue to hang around them, they will eventually dilute your willingness to excel. They will poison your mind with their own anemic sense of accomplishment. You will begin to settle for a comfort zone right beside them. You should always have a slight discontentment and a striving to make things a little better. It is healthy! It gives you purpose in life and gives you the mindset to become just a little bit better each day.

The wrong friends will hogtie your ambitions.

CHAPTER 64

THINK OF YOURSELF AS ALREADY BEING WHAT YOU WANT TO BECOME.

If you act every day as though you have already achieved your pictured goal, the transition into that very person becomes easier. It is somewhat like an actor who submerses himself into his character so that he is convincing in every detail. Sometimes, highly skilled actors actually walk like, talk like, think like, eat like, and drink like the character they want to become for their part for weeks to really "feel" the character.

As an example, if you want to become the head of a large corporation, you will have to develop command presence and appear to anyone who looks at you that you are confident, decisive, knowledgeable, and someone who people will follow. You will have to develop what is known as "gravitas". Things you say must carry some weight. You can't afford to look silly and trivial. Your conversation can't be gossipy, nor complaining, nor immature.

If you want to become an attorney, you have to always appear that you have thoroughly researched every detail of the case you are working on, and appear that you are in total control, whether you really are or not. You will always have a couple of covert moves ready to divulge at the strategic moment. You can't afford to appear to be caught by surprise.

If you want to be a journalist, you have to look and act like you will have the guts to be a bulldog and ask the difficult questions. You have to be aggressive and somewhat obnoxious and insist on getting the answers you are going after. You can't be polite and timid.

A preacher will have to look and act pious, caring, and understanding, but not silly or overly jovial, etc. You get it. You wouldn't mistake a preacher's reserved dignity for a clown with silly antics.

Every position and every field has an "aura" of behavior that is the usual and expected behavior for that field. After you decide on the hat you want to wear, that is, what you want to become, start being that person by acting like that person would act. The image is important in any pursuit. Study the aura and develop into that person.

Throughout life you will take on several "auras" as you move from one pursuit into something else. Study actors and notice how they pull off becoming their character. None of this should conflict with your personal convictions and moral behavior. Those should remain steady and be a foundation for your overall behavior.

In short, act, talk, think, and look like the person you wish to become and the mental transition into your goal persona will be more automatic.

Your view of yourself has a large influence on how you see yourself in the world, and also, how the world sees you. The other aspect of your self-image is exactly what you see yourself as doing. I heard this story from one of the great motivational speakers, and I will condense it here by paraphrasing it.

Two stonemasons were laying brick and they were working side by side. When asked what he was doing, the first stonemason said, "I am laying brick!" He viewed what he was doing as a job. He had an employee mentality and saw himself as a cog in the big wheel. The second stonemason replied differently. He said, "I am building one of the world's great cathedrals!" The difference was only in how he viewed his life and his efforts. He was inspired by his work and didn't just view it as a job. He was accomplishing something great. He was physically doing exactly the same as his co-worker, but he had a visionary grasp of his work and his life. He was doing something great because he saw the big picture and the end game. Do that for yourself and be aware that your image of yourself tells the world how trivial or how bold you really are.

Think of yourself as already being what you want to become.

CHAPTER 65

ASK THOUGHTFUL QUESTIONS AND LISTEN TO SUCCESSFUL PEOPLE.

I touched on this in precious chapters, but it astounds me that people will go to friends for advice who aren't any more successful than they are themselves. Yet, they will avoid seeking advice from the very people who have the experiences to give the most valuable advice. Asking a friend for most advice is like the blind leading the blind. It usually doesn't end well. If they are not significantly more accomplished than you are, why would their advice be worth following?

Everything I have outlined in this book is common knowledge among successful people. It is all like breathing air to them. It is second nature to them. Every one of them used some of what is in this book to attain and keep success. The behaviors I describe to become successful are very simple, but require you to get off of your butt and work pointedly for a specific thing. If expending effort is your problem, you are just plain lazy and aimless. Unless you conquer laziness, you are destined for lifelong mediocrity and struggle at best, or a life of poverty at worst. Again, maybe you just aren't miserable enough for long enough yet to be ready to make the necessary changes. Maybe you should put this book on a shelf and re-read it when your life really looks desperate, and you are serious enough to act.

If you just don't have a clue what you want in life, you have spent too much of your time on trivial pursuits and haven't disciplined your mind in deductive reasoning and decision making. You haven't given enough serious thought to who you are and where you want to go.

You learn by being observant, reading, studying, and asking questions.

Reading junk is throwing your time away. Read things that will help you.

Studying doesn't end in school. All successful people study anything relevant to their pursuits for their whole career. They will still be learning more on the day they die. Many people drone their way through life waiting to die.

Asking questions of knowledgeable people is the best way to get facts and years of experience and wisdom for free. They won't put up with trivial and silly questions from "wishers" who are looking for freebies and shortcuts. They will however, go out of their way for anyone they perceive as serious and diligent. Don't take advice from fools.

Develop a strong sense of curiosity. Investigate anything and everything that might help you. Constantly ask thoughtful questions in every conversation.

Ask yourself every day what you want until you figure it out. Every day that you don't answer that question is a day that is lost forever. In 5 years you still won't know unless you face it head on. Stop jerking around and get serious about life.

Successful people have much patience with starters like you. They were all there once.

What successful people don't have, is patience for a person who is always going to do something, but that never actually does it. Those people talk a good game, but they are not doers. They are full of excuses.

They continually fool themselves.

They say things like:

I was so busy!

I forgot!

I intend to!

I just can't decide!

I will do it soon!

I'm waiting for--------.

I don't know what to do next!

I was tired and had to take a nap!

I just haven't had the time to order that book!

I didn't want to use my day off to do anything for my future!

I don't have a player to listen to motivational tapes and CD's!

Does any of this describe you?

Ask thoughtful questions and listen to successful people

CHAPTER 66

INTRODUCE YOURSELF CONFIDENTLY WITH A MEASURED SMILE AND A MEASURED HANDSHAKE WHILE LOOKING A PERSON IN THE EYES.

As you introduce yourself to a successful person, he will begin sizing you up before you say a single word. He's just doing his job. He already has a pretty good idea about what you are by the way you carry yourself, your posture, your confidence, your handshake, your general neatness, and your ability to look him in the eyes. He's sizing you up to see how you might fit into his numerous plans. He is always looking for people or situations which can become useful and profitable. Don't be intimidated. Remember that he is just a successful person, that's all. He's not God. It means that he simply applied many of the rules in this book before you did. He still wipes his fanny with toilet paper just like you do. Most successful people are very nice, but there are a few jackasses that have a dead spot in their development. If you run into one of those, don't let it get to you. Think of them as the turd that they are, and go on to another person that is friendlier and more developed. Maybe they will fill in their inadequacies and improve some before you meet again. We are all on a continuous journey to become better.

You will do yourself a favor to work retail in some kind of store for a while. The experience of greeting people, solving their problems, and chatting with them will pay dividends your whole life. Meeting and working with people is basic to civilization itself, and it is one of the most difficult things for introverts like myself to master. It is uncomfortable for most of us, but force yourself to get over your awkwardness and force yourself to interchange. It will get easier. One of the easiest ways to break the ice is to ask questions. Ask thoughtful questions. Continue the conversation with more questions about anything that you don't fully understand. That lets the other person know you are really paying attention, and that you are interested in what they are saying. After a couple of exchanges like that, the conversation will usually take off and become more flowing.

There are a few people who just won't talk. They are the most exasperating. It is usually because of their own inadequacies. You will probably be better off just finding another person to spend your conversational energies with because your job isn't to work on them, but to improve yourself. If you have presented yourself well, and they just don't respond, politely cut off the conversation and look for a better conversational match. You won't learn much from that kind of person without undue effort. Notice how uncomfortable that kind of person makes you feel and don't do it yourself.

I have heard it said that there is virtue in just being quiet and sometimes that is true. In my experience, I have concluded that many people who are quiet really don't have much of value to say. They are literally too afraid to open their mouth.

The opposite can also be true when you run into a motor mouth that just won't stop talking. These motor mouths are never successful people. They usually talk on and on about nothing and everything without really saying much. They will waste your time. That is why I say that you should be thoughtful in your conversation and not be trivial, gossipy, or flippant. Notice how uncomfortable that kind of person makes you feel.

You don't want to be either kind.

Introduce yourself confidently with a measured smile and a measured handshake while looking a person in the eyes.

CHAPTER 67

YOU MIGHT GET A HUNDRED "NO" ANSWERS FOR EVERY "YES".

Some of the best training you will ever get is to sell some product or service that is difficult to sell. At a very early age, I sold garden seeds, my lawn services, and magazine subscriptions door to door. It was brutal! What it taught me was that many people are rude, most people are nice but simply not interested, and many people are impatient. Only a very few people really want what you were selling. It taught me two monumental lessons.

First, it taught me that it is absolutely critical to target the correct demographic by understanding the kind of people that will likely want what you are selling. In other words, if you want to sell magazines, you sell to the age groups and interest groups that read those particular magazines. You will sell more hard rock recordings to younger people, canes to older people, sporting equipment to people who care about fitness, fancy food to the people who can afford it and understand it, and luxury products like diamonds to people who can afford them. Trying to sell to the wrong demographic equates to poor sales and a low success rate.

Secondly, I learned that there will always be many more people who do not want what you have to sell than do want it. Expect it. If you make only one out of a hundred sales you will win if you just don't give up. Success is a sometimes just a numbers game. The difficulty of what you are achieving is in proportion to the number of failed attempts. If you are inventing a completely new source of energy, it is a nearly impossible task with enormous rewards. It is so difficult that the odds of success are almost insurmountable. Huge risk—huge reward. Easy goals are easy to achieve, so the success rate is much higher. Expect many failures, and many "no's", before you get a "yes". Don't let the inevitable "no's" get you down.

You have to develop a thick skin and develop resilience to the negative thoughts that creep in when you have experienced your ninety ninth "no". It is like Thomas Edison said "The difference between success and failure is that the successful person just keeps trying after the ninety ninth failure". I'm paraphrasing it, but it is absolutely true.

You might get a hundred "no" answers for every "yes".

CHAPTER 68

COLLEGE DEGREES ARE GREAT, BUT THAT IS ONLY A TINY FRACTION OF THE KNOWLEDGE THAT IS OUT THERE.

When I was newly married and had a single year of college under my belt, I started a very small plastics manufacturing business. My main clients were a couple of men a few years older than I was who were innovative and had started two businesses themselves. One was a business of manufacturing artificial inseminating equipment and electric branding irons for beef cattle. The other business was the dawn of the digital display business. My business was to design the molds and produce the prototype molded plastic parts for them.

They were both brilliant men. One of the guys had done his Master's thesis on the effects of formal education (college degrees) on financial success. He was surprised by the findings of his own study. You would expect that the more formal education and training that a person had acquired would translate into higher earnings commensurate with the level of college education. It didn't. What he found was that there were two particular groups of people who were the most financially successful.

One of the most financially successful groups are those very highly trained people with PhD degrees who had gone into business using their degrees. They generally held patents on inventions or on some production processes. Many of them had gone to work for corporations and were well off because they earned a high salary, but were not nearly as financially successful as those that had started their own businesses.

The peak of the most financially successful group consisted of people who had very little formal education. This surprised him. Most of them had less than a high school education, but they had great motivation to improve themselves and to prove themselves. They had developed grit at an early age, the capacity for self-starting, and they had developed a head for business. In short, they were entrepreneurs. They ended up starting and owning chains of stores, large apartment complexes, had real estate empires, or had a series of different and unrelated businesses. A large percentage of them were once poor and started with nothing. None of them had inherited any money.

The group that you would expect to be largely financially successful were the college graduates who learned a profession, applied it and amassed a fortune over time. That didn't happen nearly as often as he had expected. They were just comfortable enough that they considered themselves successful with their degrees and their place in society. They didn't learn grit, business skills, and just weren't hungry enough to put out the extra energy to really make things happen. They were just a little too comfortable and were content working for someone else. They didn't have aspirations of being the master of their own lives.

I have observed that most doctors and dentists are the worst possible money managers. They are highly skilled, highly educated, and very busy people. They typically have eight to twelve years of advanced training. As a group, they make large amounts of money as earnings for services go. The pressure of the responsibility of life and death decisions is mind boggling. Most of them live a very nice to lavish lifestyle, but many have never learned the things I am teaching you in this book. They had great discipline to go through school, college, medical school, specialty school, and residency. They stay so busy with so much responsibility that most of them haven't taken the time to develop the skills to make their money work passively for them. They actually make so much that they will always be comfortable, but as a group they are considered financially unsophisticated. They are a favorite mark for scammers. A few of them are not as I have described. Those few have learned financial skills and are financial dynamos in action. That few belong to the highly successful educated group. They have learned the alternative education I am conveying in this book.

So what demographic constitutes the most financially self-made successful people? The most successful group includes the poor person living paycheck to paycheck that hated their circumstance so much that they forced themselves to become better and never quit. I am in that group. Nothing in their way discouraged them enough to stop them. Do you fit into that demographic? If you do, you are a prime candidate to become financially wealthy.

Formal college education is very valuable, but our society has put entirely too much emphasis on that form of education. I am not diminishing the importance of formal education at all. I highly recommend as much of it as you can get -------BUT--------common sense, entrepreneurial skills, people skills, financial skills, and simple business skills that are practiced by every successful small business owner and entrepreneur in the country are even more important. They are outlined in the information I am giving you. This information is as important to you as all of the formal education you will ever get. These things alone will take you as far as you choose to go in life. The old saying, "You can lead a horse to water, but you can't make them drink!" is absolutely true. I am telling you what has worked for me, and I know it works. It is up to you and you alone to use it. I have led you to the water, now it is up to you to drink it.

I see one of the biggest advantages of formal education is being able to communicate on an equal level with people from any level of society. The same goes for knowing tradesman skills and blue collar skills enough to communicate with that level of person. All levels are important. Don't ever get the idea that your formal education makes you superior to a tradesman. Never underestimate anyone at any level. You should work at being able to discuss fine art and literature as comfortably as discussing how to install a septic tank or repair a car.

College degrees are great, but that is only a tiny fraction of the knowledge that is out there.

CHAPTER 69

GOOD BUSINESS IS WHEN BOTH
SIDES WALK AWAY HAPPY.

There are different theories of doing business. I don't believe in the ruthless way of doing business. Ruthless people always have to feel like they are taking advantage of others and feel like they won big at the expense of others.

Running a gemstone business for decades gave me an opportunity to exercise honor and fairness in dealing with all of my clients. I always explained the inner economics of the business and even sometimes told clients the prices I paid for some stones. I explained the difficulty in finding them, mining them, risk of cutting them, risk of transporting them, and merchandising them. It is a very long and risky trip from the jungle to my desk where I can lay them in front of clients in an air conditioned office and behind locked and secure doors. For instance, a one carat average quality diamond requires the mining of 27 tons of diamond bearing rock in a deep hole in a remote country. The many tons of diamond bearing rock are processed and then any stones found are sorted by quality and size by a classifier. Then they are shipped thousands of miles to a cutting center where they are each studied carefully and cut for maximum yield. The cutting process takes from days to months. Then they are sold to a wholesaler that carries them all over the country and sells them (usually one at a time) to a retailer. The retailer then shows them to clients and might make a sale or not. I have sold some diamonds quickly, but I have also had my money tied up in some valuable diamonds for many years without selling them. It is all a business risk with heavy expenses. Most clients could understand after an explanation that it is a business. It is sometimes is a glamorous one, but it is just a business. Every person in the supply chain has to make a legitimate profit.

Maybe it is easier to understand a head of lettuce at the grocery store. It costs about a dollar and a half at the store. Try to grow it and put it on your table for that price.

Try to imagine making your shirt which you paid ten dollars for. How many hours do you think it would take you to make it and what would it look like when you finished?

In explaining things in a practical way so that both individuals of a transaction understand the economics, a mutual equality of value received leaves each party with a good feeling and a willingness to do more business in the future.

Any time a person or a business is full of secrets, it usually means that they are trying to take advantage of you because their profit margin is unreasonable. All businesses deserve to make a fair profit, and you should make a fair profit on any transaction you ever do commensurate with the amount of effort, money expended, risk, and intellectual skill you had to expend.

Predatory business and ruthless business leaves one of the parties thinking they were taken advantage of. If only one side of a deal is happy, that is probably the last time they will do business with that same person or company. Good business is repeat business and promotes a good reputation which is necessary for a healthy business. It is not necessary or wise to be so harsh in business as to walk away with all of the cookies. It is o.k. and wise to be a tough negotiator, but there is a point of diminishing long term benefits. A quick profit gained from harsh and ruthless business practices is bad business, and it is bad karma. It will return home to bite you in the fanny.

Some businessmen disagree with me on this subject, but I really believe that what goes around, comes around. If you act with integrity, life will reward you. If you act selfishly and ruthlessly, life will punish you.

Good business is when both sides walk away happy.

CHAPTER 70

ALWAYS PERFORM A LITTLE EXTRA AND DO MORE THAN YOU PROMISE.

I have already said that it is important to make very few promises, and also, if you make them, keep them.

Now let's go just a little bit further. Keep your promises, and also, perform a little extra. If you always give a little extra, it leaves a good taste in the other persons mouth, and they will remember that you not only performed according to your word, but you went the extra mile and did even more than you said you would. That kind of performance stands out and will pay many dividends to your reputation and to your future opportunities. You will get a reputation for excellence which is worth enormous cash to you over a lifetime of doing business.

When doing business, I would always try to make the price of something just a little lower than I was contracted for. I would also let people know when I incurred more expense than planned for a contract, and would still honor a quoted price, which actually accomplishes the same thing. I would remind them, "I quoted you this price, and it actually ran 9% more. I gave you my word and I will keep the same price that we agreed on." It was always appreciated, and it resulted in future business.

If you put yourself in their shoes, how would receiving extra make you feel?

Always perform a little extra and do more than you promise.

CHAPTER 71

TRUE COMPASSION IS POWER.

There are many subtle traits that will propel you ahead in life. One of the most powerful is the ability to express compassion. What is compassion? I will quote one of my favorite motivational speakers, Zig Ziglar. He stated, "People don't care how much you know, until they know how much you care... about them." On your journey to success, it might seem like you are being selfish. You are not. The more valuable you are as a person, the more value you will have to share with the world. Your success will make the world a better place if you have compassion to help other people on your way to success. Zig Ziglar was a consummate salesman before he got into the motivational business. Now he sells people on themselves, which indeed, is a high calling. I attended one of his positive thinking seminars and purchased his motivational tapes when I was in my mid-twenties. I still use them today, and I am 74. He had a very big impact on my view of the world. Mr. Ziglar is an extremely astute student of the human condition. His understanding comes from detailed observation of what causes people to make decisions. In his days of selling very expensive pots and pans, he formulated an understanding of exactly what made people do what they do. In his case, when he wanted to sell his pots and pans, he didn't take the approach of making a sale because it would be a good thing for himself. He concerned himself genuinely that his product, which he believed in wholeheartedly, was the absolute perfect product for the needs of the person he was talking to. Do you think anyone would give him two seconds of their time if they thought he was just in it just for himself? Mr. Ziglar understood that he had to really be compassionate and really care about his customers by being interested in the benefits his pots and pans actually have on their lives. All sales work like this.

People care about themselves. They are their own favorite subject. That's not necessarily a bad thing. It is just the human condition. It isn't even particularly selfish. It is part of our survival instinct. You are far more likely to pay attention to a person that you sense really cares about you. You will be more likely to accept their ideas and opinions. If compassion is genuine, it will show. If you sense that another person doesn't care about you, it does the opposite by making you feel repelled. True compassion must be felt in order to be a force of positive power.

People will be drawn to you if you show compassion because they sense that you really care about them. I am impressed and amazed by nurses in hospitals and nursing homes that hectically work their fannies off for long hours every day. Most of them have true compassion for their patients. That compassion is actually a healing influence to the patients. I had a nurse one time who wasn't compassionate, and every time she walked in the room, it felt like Darth Vader was there. Her aura was actually poisonous. I dreaded her presence. She should quit nursing and go on to another field where she would do less damage.

Compassion is power.

CHAPTER 72

MONEY WILL DESTROY A PERSON WHO HASN'T LEARNED THE RULES OF MONEY. INHERITED MONEY IS THE MOST DANGEROUS.

Money in the hands of a person who hasn't learned the rules of money is as dangerous to that person as putting a loaded gun in the hands of a four year old child.

The way you know for sure that a person knows nothing about how money works is that they always think that if they just had a chunk of money, that all of their problems will be solved. They won't! I have had some multimillion dollar lottery winners as direct clients. I have also known about multimillion dollar lottery winners who were clients of my wholesale clients. It is pathetic to watch how they squander their easily won money. Easy come, easy go!

The same goes for people who inherit money without a fundamental knowledge of how money works. They don't understand it. They don't understand what it will do and what it won't do. They don't respect it. They don't know its deadly power. Most of all, they have never had their own skin in the game to earn chunks of it, and don't have the wisdom to put it to work. They haven't developed the self-discipline to handle it wisely. It slips through their fingers and disappears with little or nothing to show for it.

My dear father-in-law was a very intelligent farmer and investor with much wisdom and much common sense. One of his many poignant sayings was "There isn't a pond big enough that it can't be drained". Lottery winners, financially immature people who inherit money, and undisciplined people who are not inherently thrifty soon find out that the pond is drained dry.

One of my wholesale diamond dealer clients was associated with a couple who won a multimillion dollar lottery. They were paid over $440,000 at the same time every year for twenty years. That is enough money to start several businesses in a single year alone which would make their entire lineage wealthy forever if they had managed it properly. Instead, since they lived in a single wide trailer, they bought a new double wide trailer, bought an above ground swimming pool, bought new cars and trucks, bought sports vehicles, bought an expensive boat rig, spent lavishly on foo foo junk, bought flashy but not substantial jewelry from my wholesale client, and gambled the rest away in Biloxi, Mississippi casinos. Each year, entire $440,000 was gone in a couple months, and they were broke for the rest of the year until the next big check came in. After a couple months they were back in my client's office selling back the jewelry to him at a steep loss to raise enough money to continue their deadly spending for a while longer. Throughout the rest of the year, they sold off vehicles for a fraction of the price they had paid. That was the way they thought millionaires lived! They were hooked on the feeling they got when they acted out their version of rich and irresponsible. They repeated the cycle year after year. They didn't know that most millionaires work many hours managing their investment holdings and businesses. Soon the lottery winner's money pond will be dry, and it is likely that they will become suicide statistics like so many fools are.

I had a client who was an old man when I dealt with him. (Actually he was about the age I am now!) He was a good worker all his life and made a living in the insurance business, but never had any chunks of money. My client, who was in his seventies, inherited a small fortune from an uncle. He never had any financial experience so he didn't know what to do with the money. He was almost afraid of it so he entrusted it to a religious organization to manage it for him. He didn't attempt to learn anything himself about investments and thought it would be safe because the organization was tied to a church promising a sizeable return. When he told me the high rate of promised return (somewhere around 12%), it raised a red flag. Just as I thought, it turned out to be a Ponzi scheme, and he lost it all. His benefactor had worked and managed well for many years to amass that money, and he squandered it because of his financial ignorance. The financial pond was dry.

Another client and his wife inherited a medium sized fortune. They were both nice people, but they were financially unsophisticated and accustomed to working for a salary. They had never invested money and didn't have a clue what to do with it. They learned just enough about the stock market to speak the lingo and seem impressive to people who didn't know much. They were a little foggy about short positions, index funds, and about derivatives, but they used these terms that they thought they understood. To a novice they sounded like they knew what they were doing, but they didn't. As soon as they left our office, I told my wife that they would be broke in a year. I was wrong! It took a little over a year and a month, and they were back to living on their lives on their salaries. They had lost it all. The financial pond was dry. They never mentioned the stock market again.

We once purchased a small acreage from a person who had a pedigreed lineage. I had a difficult time figuring this person out because he was very unpredictable. Something about him just didn't fit. He made puzzling financial decisions and always bought everything on credit. He was near foreclosure on two expensive houses. He also never finished projects to completion, and always had too many things going simultaneously. Secretly, I questioned his financial judgment. One day as we were discussing the economy, he told me that he had invested his entire savings in a managed fund that was paying a very high interest rate with a zero downside guarantee. That is impossible! Legitimate business just can't guarantee zero downside, and the only reason for high interest rates is if the venture or fund carries a large risk. Any time you see something like this, run from it as fast as you can. My red flag went up again. I asked him how he thought it was possible for the fund to pay more interest than everybody else and guarantee no losses, but he just brushed it aside and said that he was getting his big interest checks regularly so he wasn't worried. I asked him, "What about the principal?" and he said that he didn't intend to touch the principal. He had no exit plan. His only concern was the big interest income he was getting in quarterly checks. I warned him that the fund had all the earmarks of a Ponzi scheme and told him that his principal would likely disappear into somebody's Swiss bank account and not be returned to him—ever. All he will get is the interest, but very likely lose his principal. He will likely never see his principal again, and he was very likely fleeced. He died a few years later, and his heirs will likely soon have a big surprise. It is just as well, because the heirs were also financially unsophisticated. They would likely soon lose it. What a shame. Remember old Ben Franklin. "A fool and his money are soon parted."

Money is a sacred tool. It has to be respected for its positive power, and also, be respected and feared for its ability to woo people into foolish behavior. Inherited money leaks out like water leaking from a bucket with a small hole in it. It dribbles out in tiny amounts in order to boost the ego of the fool who is spending it. Pretty soon the financial pond is dry. The money is gone, and you can't even identify why it is gone or where it went. It is gone because you didn't keep track of the first rule---- keep track of everything you make and spend—in writing. Financially ignorant people don't realize how ignorant and foolish they are. People who go through life just making a living on wages their whole life are financially ignorant. Re-read CHAPTER 35 to review many of the important rules of money.

Money will destroy a person who hasn't learned the rules of money. Inherited money is the most dangerous.

CHAPTER 73

THE FIRST $10,000 IS THE HARDEST TO MAKE. IT IS YOUR SEED MONEY.

There are countless ways to earn and save $10,000 if you have the discipline to live below your means and save consistently from every paycheck. You can earn it flipping hamburgers at MacDonald's for minimum wage, or you can earn it by practicing law as an attorney. It might take considerably longer in a low paying job, but it can be done and is done by many immigrants who come to this country. Many of them can see and take advantage of the enormous opportunities that we have in our culture while many born here are blind to them. They seem to recognize it quicker than people raised in America because that opportunity is in contrast to much less opportunity they saw in their birth country.

The secret is not in how much you make, it is in how much you don't spend. I loaded myself down with the responsibilities of a family at a young age, and it took me longer than it will probably take you to get your seed money, but I did it, none the less, in a large part because I married a wife that shared my goals and ambitions and shared my discipline of money. A mate that doesn't share responsible financial values with you will keep you broke forever. Consistency in paying into your seed money savings fund is more than important. It is critical! After you put the seed money to work, it will begin to generate money easier and easier as you develop your investing and business skills.

I will repeat some things I have already said because they are so important.

Focus like a laser on acquiring your seed money. Don't buy anything that is not absolutely necessary until you get started, and you are stable. If you spend all of your money to live well and have loads of fun when you are young, you will sabotage the rest of your life. You might even end up bagging groceries standing on your feet all day at the age of sixty or seventy. You can see many of those people every time you go to the grocery store. You can do better for yourself.

If you use financial discipline, your future can include traveling, driving a fine car, eating filet mignon and lobster, living at a good standard, and being able to buy and do anything you want to do or need to do. IF YOU LEARN HOW TO CREATE PASSIVE INCOME STREAMS, YOUR $100 BILLS WILL NEVER RUN OUT! All you have to do is learn and use responsible money skills. Once you learn to make a fortune, you never forget it, and you can repeat it at any time if you lose it in some bad investment. That first $10,000 of seed money is the key. Treat it as the most important goal in your life until you make it and put it to work for you.

The first $10,000 is the hardest to make. That's your seed money.

CHAPTER 74

ONCE YOU LEARN THE RULES OF MAKING MONEY, THEN LEARN HOW TO KEEP IT AND MAKE IT GROW.

I made the previous chapter about the simplicity of accumulating your $10,000 in seed money. Now you have your money in your hot little hand and can't wait to put it to work. You are holding the financial equivalent of a loaded gun in your hand unless you have burned the rules of money into your brain.

You are having mixed feelings because you worked and saved carefully, and you don't want to make a mistake and lose it all.

Grandpa, I have my seed money, now what do I do with it? That is the question I hope my grandkids are asking about now.

Have you been using your time wisely to do detailed research on each possible place to put your money to work while you were earning and saving your seed money? If not, you are not ready to proceed.

Have you consulted people in the field or investment you are considering?

Have you talked to several successful people in general and gotten a feel for how they approach their ventures? How they think?

Have you discussed the economics of your venture with people accustomed to handling money?

Have you listed all pros and cons of each possible business venture or investment– IN WRITING? Have you asked all necessary questions? Have you answered each and every question to ease any doubts that were lingering?

Have you crunched all of the numbers and have a grasp of all financial factors?

Have you written a business or investing plan? IN WRITING? What is your entrance strategy? What is your production or dwell time strategy for your venture or business? What is your exit strategy?

If you are missing any of this information, you have two choices:

Choice 1— Close your eyes and just throw the seed money you earned at something that feels good. Maybe it's something that you or a close friend just have a hunch about. If you make this choice, be ready to admit this first mistake when you lose your seed money. You'll do it right next time by making Choice 2.

Choice 2— Take a deep breath, go back and reassure yourself that you are truly convinced that you have covered everything you can. Review all of your notes. Now, go back and do everything on the list above. Make absolutely sure you have considered everything.

Now, go forward with confidence and resolve that you WILL make your venture work! Resolve to tend it like a newborn baby, because that is exactly what you have. A venture or business will need daily attention. Resolve to yourself that you will not give up—ever. Resolve that FAILURE IS ABSOLUTELY NOT AN OPTION. Watch for early signs that things aren't going as planned and be ready to correct them. Be vigilant for minor or major changes in conditions that warrant your judgment call. I hope you are still consulting someone you have come to trust that really knows what they are doing. Don't panic, don't second guess yourself, and don't get discouraged. You will be just fine, and your money will soon start to work for you if you have covered everything correctly.

The exact thing you choose to do is not the important thing. You can make just as much money selling tires as you can by selling insurance or selling groceries. You can make as much by starting almost any business if you did all of your homework to research it and then run it well. What is important is how you have prepared yourself with the knowledge you will need to make it a success. Nearly anything CAN be successful if you do it well enough. The same goes for investments.

This all sounds very complicated, but after you do it one time, it will become automatic and you will develop what is called a "business head". You will soon get so that the whole process becomes automatic. Then, most of it just becomes how you think and see the world. You will have developed an entrepreneurial mindset. People who have an employee mentality don't think in terms of running a business. They think in terms of making a fixed amount of money for their time. They will always be employees. They will have a J.O.B. and be Just Over Broke if they keep their employee mentality. It is even likely that you will be employing some of them in the future. These exercises will help you develop an employer mentality and an investor mentality by helping you to develop a good business head. You will have become a successful entrepreneur.

Now that you have planted your first batch of seed money somewhere that is making money, you need to decide your strategy to either run businesses as income generators, start businesses and then sell them as income generators, or primarily make your money with partially or fully passive investments. I personally have used three of the four.

I personally loved the wholesale and retail rare gemstone and jewelry business for a number of reasons. Those two businesses have been my mainstay as an active venture for decades. They continued to provide seed money for several other ventures. The other ventures were a combination of active and passive ventures and generated income in different ways. They included land and other real estate which then generated even larger chunks of cash. Many of the world's fortunes have been generated by earnings from real estate investment. Rare collectibles are highly lucrative if you know enough about each field. I have earned significant money from them. The collectible could be porcelain dolls, stamps, coins, antiques, glassware, artwork, cars, tools, baseball cards, autographs, rare books, period clothing, paperweights, gemstones, mineral specimens, or just about anything that people can collect. They are almost a passive investment because you just have to buy right, and then decide when to sell them. Knowing the details of each specific collectible field is paramount. The learning curves are costly while you are becoming an expert in any given field.

It had served me well to always have a solid business which generated significant income. Enough income so that large chunks of money could be earned through business dealings and then invested in other ventures. I still always had the security of the base businesses. If some of those other ventures didn't work out as planned, I still had the base businesses to rely on to generate further seed money quickly. At one time we lost almost two million dollars that would have devastated us if we didn't have the base businesses to rely on to recover. We bought several very expensive waterfront building lots and vacation houses that initially rapidly escalated in value. The insurance industry decided to stop insuring houses or building loans in that area because it was less than 10 feet above sea level. That made it nearly impossible to sell the properties. Very few people had the cash to fund a project without borrowed money. Then the 2008 decline dropped the market and nothing would sell. We rode the market down to bottom. What saved us was diversified investments and a base business.

I always kept ready cash available to take advantage of anything that crossed my path that could turn a good profit. If anything came along that I could buy below market and roll over for a quick profit, I was all over it. Sometimes the profit was slower. As an example, I bought an airplane for $28,000 from an old man, we flew it all over the country and sold it for $46,000 nine years later. It actually became a passive investment and I had free use of it for 9 years. During that 9 years I ran into other airplanes that would have been just as good of a passive investment. We found a medium sized twin engine jet we could have bought for $250,000 in a distressed sale. At the time I just wasn't comfortable going after it, but it was a money maker. Good deals are everywhere, but you need chunks of cash and adequate knowledge to recognize them and make them work.

The ultimate goal is to generate passive investment streams. Those are places to put your money where the investment or venture is on autopilot, and you just collect the earnings or profit without much further effort.

In the old days, particularly in wealthy families, "coupon clipping" was and to some degree still is, the primary way to generate passive income. Coupon clipping is slang for investing in stocks that pay a consistent dividend. I won't get into the detailed specifics for why I don't believe in this method for lowly millionaires (with single digit millions), but it is primarily due to the reality of double digit inflation and the crookedness of the banking industry and stock market as I explained in CHAPTER 13. That area of investing is really geared more to the billionaire types. They have enough money and power to manipulate the market, and also, have inside information that you and I don't have access to. If you chose to invest there, be ready for some really serious surprises and some very scary roller coaster rides. I found out that my shares could be nullified and replaced by shares of insiders, making my shares worthless. I found out that if you own shares in a company, they can force you to sell at a fixed price even though you don't want to sell after they acquired a merger that would make the stock explode in value. I found out that as soon as you start to make serious money using a trading platform with published rules, the big boys can, and do, change the rules so that only they can take advantage of all market conditions, but deny the same privileges to you. I found out that the big boys can and regularly do, institute huge computer generated trades where the buy and sell is executed in microseconds which triggers both long and short stops on positions which robs the investor/traders of their money. This is done almost daily. These tricks cost me hundreds of thousands of dollars. It was a costly lesson.

I do know several people personally that have made serious money on the stock market. Some have even held on to their money. Many have not. It requires being married to a computer to watch your stock prices constantly which is not the way I want to spend my time.

My father-in-law), had invested in the Chicago Board of Trade and traded commodities for many years. He had come to the same conclusion that I did many years later. It is a rigged game which is stacked in the favor of the biggest investors. The little guy doesn't stand a chance. His comment after many years of experience was "I'll tell ya', the stock market and commodity market is just like gambling in a Las Vegas casino. The average guy doesn't stand a chance."

The moral of this story is:

The more you know about a venture or an investment, the more successful you will be, and the less likely it is for you to lose money.

Once you learn the rules of making money, then learn how to keep it and make it grow.

CHAPTER 75

THINK BIG AND DON'T LET THE LITTLE THINGS DIVERT YOU

I have been guilty of thinking too small. Particularly, after we attained a degree of financial success. I didn't realize how much our changed circumstances had expanded our possibilities. That is one of the regrets I have in life. I guess in the end it won't matter much, because making more money past the point of stability and security is a moot point. You can only wear one pair of pants at a time, and you don't need many houses to live in. I like driving 10 year old cars because I don't like to scratch the paint on a new one, and I don't like the depreciation on a new one. The added disadvantage of having even more money than is practical is that you have to worry even more about the irresponsible way some of your heirs will destroy themselves with it if they inherited it before they have learned the rules of money. I'm still deciding what to do with it. Let's see if this book makes any difference.

While you are building your fortune, think big. Don't sweat the small stuff that competes for your attention. Life is full of diversions that take attention away from your mission. Keep in mind that as you progress financially and progress in proficiency, you will expand your opportunities to accomplish more. Keep thinking in terms of stretching your comfort zone. It keeps you sharp. Don't get complacent.

You should actually plan some hobbies, diversions, and downtime into your lifestyle. A life without them is dull, and you will wake up one day and not have any interests if you don't cultivate them throughout your life. Just don't let them distract you from your long term goals. Use them for recreation, rejuvenation, and for rounding out your personality.

If you follow the suggestions in the previous chapters, you won't really have any problem staying focused. If you have read this far in this book, you are already at least partially on board. I can't imagine anyone who would turn his or her back on easy directions to become wealthy and successful. Can you?

Think big and don't let the little things divert you.

CHAPTER 76

COMMIT PUBLICLY TO YOUR GOALS, AND IT WILL FORCE YOU TO WORK HARDER TOWARD THEM AND NOT FAIL

If you do everything in secret, you can cop out on your goals and nobody will ever know. It gives you the "out" that losers are always looking for.

Be bold and commit to your close friends and relatives exactly what you have in mind. I have one son who knew at a very young age that he wanted to go to a military academy, wanted to be in computers, have a family, and be successful. Everybody around him knew it because he was very vocal about it. He has done all of those things and more. He made his goals public, and there was never a doubt in his or anyone else's mind that he would accomplish every one of his goals. He is still growing and accomplishing because he knows just where he wants to go and how to get there. Is that because he has superpowers? No, it is because he knows how to commit, work hard, use self-discipline, and he refuses to accept failure. He has the same kind of minor flaws that all of us have, but he knows how to commit and how to follow up.

Every successful person that I know commits to their goals publicly so they can't cop out in a weak moment. There will be weak moments. You just have to stay the course. Committing publicly puts the pressure on you to simply NOT allow yourself to fail. After all, how would it look if you commit publicly and then fail to perform?

I know several people who live pretty secret lives because they know they don't have self-discipline to do what they attempt. They build a mechanism for failure into their life strategy. They keep their ambitions and plans secret. You know some of them. They start many things, but rarely complete them.

They have fleeting ideas that sound good to them at the moment, but they don't have the resolve to see them through. They never even come close to being their best selves because they lack commitment. They usually have short relationships or have multiple divorces in their past. They let their vices rule their lives and can't focus. In short–they lack commitment and they are ruled by fear! Part of the advantage in committing publicly to your goals is to observe the reaction of other successful people to your intentions.

Commit publicly to your goals, and it will force you to work harder toward them and not fail.

CHAPTER 77

EVERYTHING IS NEGOTIABLE

All relationships are constant negotiations. All business is a pliable series of negotiations. Learn the skills of negotiating and use it in everything you do.

In the world at large, negotiations are an everyday thing. In every foreign country I have ever been to, literally everything is negotiated openly and vigorously. From deciding the price of a cab fare, the price of a hotel room, or the price of any consumer article, negotiating is a way of life. You are considered weak and naïve' if you are not skilled at negotiating. It is expected that you vigorously negotiate everything. You are also not respected if you pay the asking price for anything without negotiating.

I was in Bangkok, Thailand to meet my contact for Burmese rubies. In those days Burma was communist and the jungle people traded uncut rubies from the Mogok mines to Thai and Chinese dealers through the Golden Triangle. It was usually done in barter for practical things they couldn't get such as motorcycle parts, tools, or other practical goods that were in short supply. It is a very dangerous place governed by drug lords who required fees for anyone passing through. If any problem or question arises, they shoot first. My contact was killed coming back out with the rubies I flew all the way to Bangkok to buy. I had to find another viable contact or my trip halfway around the world would have been for nothing. Through an international merchant, I got the general location of a Chinese family who had been in the ruby cutting business for over a century. I hadn't dealt with traditional Chinese before, but I knew that traditional Chinese held age and experience in high regard. I finally located the younger generation of the family and attempted to negotiate with him. As is customary, I was tested by being offered some synthetic stones, then some treated stones, and then a few genuine but overpriced low quality stones to see if I knew anything. The room had a simple bare concrete floor, two simple wooden chairs and a simple table. Absolutely no other décor. The Chinese don't display wealth and I like that. The dance lasted about an hour and I was getting nowhere. I finally thanked him politely and started to stand insisting very politely that I meet "Grandfather". I knew enough about Chinese culture that I would continue getting nowhere without paying homage to him. After much insistence and several polite refusals, that since grandfather didn't speak English, he would not meet with me. I politely and repeatedly insisted by saying that is O.K. because I didn't speak Chinese, but I had come a long distance to pay respect to Grandfather and buy rubies. The grandson finally reluctantly disappeared for a few minutes and returned with Grandfather. He was a short, bowed over, shuffling, and kind looking Chinese man in traditional Chinese attire. I instantly liked him. I greeted him with a sincere, respectful bow and his grandson translated my honored sentiment to him. Immediately the games stopped and he said a few words in Chinese to his grandson. His words were the approval for his grandson to start showing the real stuff to me and instantly the beginning negotiating prices fell by over 50%. He brought out rubies that I had only heard of. They were some of the finest pigeon blood stones I had ever seen and some of them were over 10 carats which for a ruby is enormous. We are talking about stones with high five digit price tags at the cutter. I still have one of the best but small stones that I was shown. I have used it for decades as is my grading stone for top pigeon blood color. I had to meet the real man in charge. My point in this tale is twofold. First, you have to think like the person you are negotiating with and honor what is important to them before you can begin to make a good deal. Secondly, you have to deal with the man in charge, not an underling.

In the United States, things like the price of a house, the price of a car, the price of a construction project, medical bills, or the interest rate and the terms of a loan are routinely negotiated. The possibility of negotiating other things is largely ignored by our culture. Young people in our culture are taught to pay the asking price for everything. Most of them don't have negotiating skills. It is only the business savvy ones who know that they can save many thousands of dollars by talking directly to the person with the authority to change the price or terms for the deal you are interested in. Learn to identify the person in charge and insist on dealing with them. Ask for the person with the authority to make the decisions. Politely insist on it like I did with the Chinese Grandfather! Don't waste your time with underlings because they have been trained to stonewall you. Their answer will always be "no!" Part of their job is to keep negotiators away from the boss. You must always insist on dealing with the person in charge. Then, you must convince them that you want to do business with them and that you are a "no hassle" person. Then, show them the cash. (Here is one of the places where chunks of money are powerful.)

It is standard business for car dealerships to have salesmen on the front line whose job it is to get as much of your money as you will part with. They consent to go to the manager to drop the price a little more only after they have reached an impasse with you. In the car business it is referred to as the "sales manager routine". This goes back and forth with "no's!" and small concessions until you ultimately stand up, politely say, "Thank you for working with me, but I just can't pay that price." and measuredly walk out the door. If they really want to do business, they will stop you and finish the deal. This is where you must really be ready to walk away or finish the deal and be ready on the spot to pay. These guys are pros, and they sense any hint of a lack of skill on your part.

I have dealt with a lot of Jewish people in my career in the precious stone business. As a group, they are very business savvy. They commonly say "Never pay retail for anything! If you don't buy it wholesale, don't buy it." The bigger the deal, the more the negotiation. I respect their business acumen, and they tend to be very successful business people. The ones I have dealt with are skilled negotiators, are very family oriented, have a strong sense of fairness, and are careful with their money. They keep their money working at all times. That is one of the reasons there are so many financially successful Jewish people

I negotiate discounts in retail stores, I negotiate terms and interest rates on loans with banks and finance companies, I negotiate contract details on real estate, I negotiate payoff balances on mortgages, I negotiate prices on virtually everything in business. I negotiate prices of cars, boats, ATV's, and airplanes. I negotiate settlements from insurance companies, I negotiate prices of operations with individual doctors, I negotiate terms of jobs with workers, I negotiate salaries, I negotiate fees with professionals such as attorneys, and I negotiate lease contracts on office space. Don't ever do any business without negotiating. If someone won't negotiate with you, don't do business with them and find someone who will negotiate. I NEGOTIATE EVERYTHING.

Part of the skill in negotiations is determining exactly what the other person considers important. Find out what is the most important to them and what isn't as important. It is as true of relationship negotiations as it is for business negotiations. In personal relationships, is it division of labor, attention, sexual differences, demonstration of respect, communication, personal habits, money management, religious beliefs, hygiene, or personal discipline that is the issue? In business, is it only the price, is it terms, is it saving face and looking good, is it respect, is it a feeling of superiority and dominance, is it the game and act of negotiating itself, or is it the cultural need to appear "macho"? Price is only a small part of negotiation in business. Learn what it is that the other side wants more than anything, and you will become a skilled negotiator in time and with some practice. That is true in relationship negotiations as well as business negotiations. In most deals you can trade off something that is minimally important to you for something much more important to you. At the same time the other person gets what is most important to them.

I once got the price on a house reduced by $5,000 by insisting that the seller of the house include his green bodied yellow nape Amazon parrot in the deal. My demand was so far out in left field that he was surprised and insulted that I wanted his parrot in the deal. Immediately, he focused on the parrot. He easily agreed to reduce the price by $5,000, but insisted that the parrot was not part of the deal. In his mind, he won. This tactic is called "diversion". It is one of many effective tactics. I would have taken the parrot, but I really didn't care one way or the other about it. He did. He wanted to keep his parrot. I just wanted a diversion to reduce the price. In our minds, we each got what was most important to us in the deal. In my mind, that parrot cost him $5,000. In his mind, he saved his parrot.

There are many books on negotiation, and you MUST read some of them. One of my favorites is "Winning Through Intimidation" by Robert Ringer. Another one is "The Negotiating Game" by Chester L. Karrass.

I hope I can talk to each one of my grandkids face to face about negotiating as they learn business skills, and I hope they ask a lot of questions about it. There are so many nuances they need to know about negotiation that it would fill many volumes of books to list them.

Diplomats determine the affairs of nations every day with their negotiating skills. The lack of understanding the fine nuances of negotiating can and do start wars. Negotiation is one of the most valuable skills you will ever learn.

Another thing about negotiation that is important to know. Everything changes with time. An offer on real estate or the rent on an office space may be rejected one day, but with the changing situation of the other person, the same offer is often accepted at another time. I once allowed an office space to remain vacant for over a year before I went back to the leasing company with the exact same previously rejected offer. Over a year later it was accepted. The original leasing agent had a Caesar's complex and had her pride tied up in the deal. Pride is a very common fatal mistake in negotiation. When she was out of the picture, I pointed out the many thousands of dollars the leasing company had already lost by not leasing it to me the year before. A much cooler head prevailed this time, and the new and wiser agent jumped at the deal. I got the office space for my price and terms. Time had passed, and the unskilled agent with the Caesar's complex was out of the picture. We stayed in that space for 23 years and paid many thousands of dollars per year to the leasing company.

Always follow up on rejected deals because conditions are always changing. People's financial circumstances change continually. I have purchased several real estate properties advantageously by doing that. What is intolerable one day can look pretty good on another day due to changing circumstances.

I have been amazed at the number of people that will negotiate the trivial things such as a trinket at a flea market or yard sale item for pennies, but will not even try to negotiate the interest rate on a major loan or the price of a car. Just a ¼ % interest on a $100,000 loan is $250 per year!! On a ten year loan that might be as much as $2,500 you saved by simply insisting on a ¼% reduction in interest. Try getting a full 2 percent reduction first and negotiate down from there if you have to. You'd be surprised at what banks or individuals will sometimes take. Also, people are more comfortable in dealing with the levels of numbers they use every day than larger numbers which intimidate them. They may be perfectly at ease dealing with $10 or even $100, but when the numbers get into the $1,000's, they choke up. Don't be intimidated by numbers.

Always reach for more than you really expect to get. It has been proven in negotiation statistics that the person who asks for more will end up with a more favorable finally negotiated settlement than the one who just tries for a nominal amount. The person who makes smaller increments of concessions will also have the edge in negotiations. If the asking price is $20,000 and you think that is o.k., try for $14,700. You might make an offer a little below a neat round figure, of say, $15,000 because the other person is really expecting you to offer about $18,000, and will initially be shocked at the $14,700 offer. The off round number always seems to unbalance them. After he catches his breath and realizes you are serious, but you are a tough negotiator, he will be much more likely to try and settle, finally, on say $16,000 after you have increased your offer in smaller and smaller increments with each of his counter offers. It might go like this: asking price $20,000, your counter $14,700 (he acts shocked and insulted), his counter $18,000, your counter $15,300, his counter $17,000, your counter $15,500, his counter $16,500, your counter "o.k., my final offer is $16,000 cash". Be ready to show them the cash. Each offer and counter offer is accompanied by the proper squirming and wincing facial expressions and excuses as to why you just are not able to pay more. This process might take a few minutes or a couple of hours. I have had many, many offers accepted for much less than I thought I could ever get as a final price. Never negotiate without the cash to back it up or you will be labeled a fool. In the business world this negotiating is called "the dance". Practice on everything and learn it well. It will save you hundreds of thousands of dollars over a lifetime. Think through your real final price, and WALK AWAY if you don't get it. In your assessment, consider all ramifications of the deal. Don't get married to a deal unless you absolutely must make it. If you must make the deal, don't let it show. Use your best poker face and be convincing. People can sense when you are desperate, and also sense when you want the deal badly. There are always more deals out there, and you will miss some deals that you regret, but that's just business. Accept it, and go on to the next one. If you show too much attachment, you will be out negotiated.

Negotiating skills take time to master, but it is absolutely vital that you develop them in your personal life and in your business life. Your marriage will depend on them and your financial well-being will depend on them. In personal negotiations as well as in business negotiations, both parties should be able to walk away with a good feeling that they got the most important thing that they wanted in the deal.

Everything is negotiable.

CHAPTER 78

FEAR—IT IS PARALYZING. IT IS BY FAR THE BIGGEST ENEMY OF SUCCESS

In some of the darkest hours of World War II, Winston Churchill gave a rallying speech to the people of England. In his famous speech he said, "The only thing we have to fear is fear itself!"

Fear keeps us from accomplishing anything worthwhile in life if we allow it to rule us. Only we, ourselves, can control its effect on us. The power to change that is in us, alone. Other people cannot erase our fears.

Most people are afraid of failing. Their fear is trying, failing, and looking bad. They simply don't want to end up looking foolish or stupid. We rationalize incorrectly that the safe thing is to do nothing. If a baby did that, he would never leave his crib, never learn how to crawl, never learn how to walk, and he would never learn how to run. He would literally live and die in his crib without experiencing anything outside the bars of his prison. He would die without really living. We are all bound by the prison of fear that we set for ourselves by allowing ego, pride, and self-doubt, to stop us from achieving the greatest self that we are all capable of.

Everything we have ever done in life involves some unknown. Life itself is unpredictable. Successful people simple accept that as fact. They don't let their ego control them and boldly just "do it".

Every time you stretch out of your comfort zone and do something different and unfamiliar, you are engaging brain circuits that continue to expand their interconnectivity. It makes each new experience easier and easier until pretty soon, what seemed impossibly uncomfortable becomes routine, and you are ready to expand your realm some more. It is called personal growth. Have you known someone who was filled with either so much self-doubt that they simple couldn't function? I know some people like that. They live tragic lives. On the other end of the spectrum, I know of others that have such inflated egos that they are actually terrified of trying and failing. They can't stand the thought of looking bad, so they just settle for mediocrity. They believe their precious ego remains intact, and they will appear to never fail. The paradox is that their greatest failure is already obvious to the world. They are ruled by their inflated ego, and they are showing it glaringly to the world in the form of not achieving what they are capable of. That is really what makes them look foolish. If they would just drop the ego, they would succeed at some things and fail at some things. After a success or two, they could build on those successes, learn from the failures, and get more and more proficient at success. They could leave the inflated ego in the rear view mirror because that inflated ego is their enemy. Their ego robs their success. Until they manage to get it under control, they will continue to be failures.

I have had many fears and self-doubts in my life. I have handled them by simply forcing myself to take the first step and starting. Take the first step, and follow that by the second, and then the third. I have found that after you start to build momentum, you lose focus on the fear that paralyzes you, and focus on the accomplishment instead. The fears are almost always an exaggeration in our mind. The only thing that gives them credence is our own biased perceptions. Inaction breeds fear. The fear grows until it is overwhelming. Don't allow that mental game to paralyze you. ACT!—GET UP AND GET GOING, and much of the fear goes away.

Fear—It is paralyzing. It is by far the biggest enemy of success.

CHAPTER 79

LAZINESS—THE SECOND BIGGEST ENEMY OF SUCCESS

Laziness applies to both body and mind.

The human mind and the human body are individually creatures of habit. Both the mind and body have inertia. If each is active, it tends to remain active. If each is stagnant, it tends to remain stagnant. The longer the mind or the body is not active, the more difficult it is to change the ingrained habit that it has become accustomed to.

Much is made of physical laziness, but mental laziness is often overlooked.

If you have allowed your mind to become lazy by droning through life and just getting by, your body will follow. You are on your decline to mediocrity and then on the road to complete failure. Is that where you are now? Is that where you want to be?

A good test for yourself to test your own level of laziness is to ask the following questions: When was the last time you had a serious conversation with someone who was an expert in any field? When is the last time you read a book to learn new knowledge about anything and not just for mindless entertainment? When is the last time you watched YouTube videos that were instructional rather than watching people or animals do stupid and dangerous things? When is the last time you started a project which required multiple efforts over a long period of time? When is the last time you sought advice from a qualified person? The final and most important one— When is the last time you actually gave really serious thought to your long term future AND came to at least one conclusion about what you were going to do about it to make it better? Get the picture? Don't be that person who wakes up when they hit age thirty and is essentially where they were at age twenty. That same person will also wake up at age forty, and still be in the same place as they were at twenty, with a few more toys and a very few serious accomplishments to their credit.

You will become what your mind thinks about the most. If you fill it with trivia, garbage, mediocrity, self-doubt, or worries, you will become a trivial, trashy, mediocre, self-doubting, non-achieving, and worried person. Is that someone you would like to be around or to marry?

How about the contrast with someone who does not have a lazy mind?

That person has thought seriously about where they are headed and has made the decisions necessary to take them there. In addition to thinking about some fun things, they think about serious things. They think about elevated pursuits, they conquer self-doubt by facing it. They have goals, and they are achieving them with action. They don't worry because they know just where they are going so their future is more secure. Is that someone you would like to be around or to marry? If you wouldn't want to marry this kind of person, then you are lazy, and you might be afraid because they might make your lazy ass look bad.

If you have a lazy mind, sooner or later you will also have a lazy body, and you will have very little success at anything you do.

If you have an active mind, you will sooner or later have an active body, and you will be successful at most things you do.

Don't make excuses. Just get off of your butt and "do it".

Laziness— The second biggest enemy of success

CHAPTER 80

INDECISION—THE THIRD BIGGEST ENEMY OF SUCCESS

In the conversations I have already had with my grandkids, the one thing that seems to be a major problem for them is that in our society is very much over communicated with the wrong things. In my grandkids' world there is twenty four hour news reporting, the internet, video games, incessant and largely inane cellphone communication with friends, social media, a sense of incompetency by our leaders and the direction our country, the threat of war, the threat of terrorist attack, bio-threats, and a general feeling of being left behind the curve in an exponentially changing world. These things are all very real, and they ARE terrifying and intimidating.

At the height of the cold war, we had duck and cover drills regularly in our schools because the threat of nuclear war was even more immediate than it is today. We had daily fears of having the flesh evaporated off of our bones at all times from a nuclear blast. We had the threat of induction into the military draft to fight and die in a futile war in Vietnam.

My parents had the immediate threat of induction into the military to fight and die in WWII and Korea. Millions did fight and die. They had the great depression from the stock market crash of 1929 and literal starvation to worry about. That was their childhood.

My grandparents had the threat of induction to fight and die in WWI. Millions fought and died in that war also. They were the parents with kids to take care of in the great depression with no jobs and few choices.

Hundreds of years ago, young men had to worry about being kidnapped and forced into service aboard sailing ships or being sold into servitude. Young women had no rights, and many were sold into slavery or servitude and molested. Child slavery and forced child labor was the norm.

So it goes, on and on, throughout history. There is always something that can be used as an excuse for not making plans and working toward them if you allow uncertainty to control your life. In all generations there are also individuals that decided to take charge of their destiny, and they directed their own futures.

The major factor I see about youth today is because of the over communication, they are aware of more trivial things that really don't matter.

The knowledge base in all fields is expanding too fast for them to comprehend and keep up, and they have so, so, many choices and options that they find it impossible to narrow down to a few choices for a life pursuit. There are just too many options. It is overwhelming to them. They have never been instructed on the skill of decision making.

Indecision seems to be a common problem for the millennial generation because they know a great many things, and have an overwhelming diversity of options. They can't make the necessary decision about what to do with their lives. They haven't developed the common sense and deductive reasoning skills yet to know how to sift through the bewildering choices that are presented to them. They are presented with more choices than any generation in history. In short, many can't make decisions efficiently and effectively—YET.

Let's use some common sense reasoning to narrow down that dazzling array of choices to a manageable course of action.

What are your three favorite interests? Why?

What activities do you find the most rewarding? Why?

Narrow down your choices to three choices of something you can use to make a rewarding career. Can you attain a high pay level with continued room for advancement which allows significant money for investment, or can each choice be used instead to attain your seed money to start a business of your own? If each choice passes this first test, go on to the next.

What specifically do you need to do to become a leader in each of the three different choices? Do they require college? Do they require technical school? Do they require trade school? Do they require apprenticeships? Do they require social and sales skills? Do they require business skills?

What kind of time and money commitment is required to become a leader in each of those choices?

Are you willing to make that money commitment and time commitment for what you choose?

If you are now willing to make those commitments, exactly what do you need to do to start getting yourself set up on a course of action to get the training or education you will need?

These three choices should be logged on paper with all of the associated information for comparison to each other. Judge each one for pro's and con's. You will soon see that the bewildering choices that kept you from deciding will fall away from your focus, and your picture of the things that really do matter to you will start to appear out of the fog of indecision. If you go down one path and see that it really isn't what you anticipated, then choose the second path and try that, and so on, and so on. If the first three all fail to pass scrutiny, then work up three more and repeat. You WILL get to a final decision if you keep working at it.

All this exercise does is to turn nebulous thoughts into concrete actions.

Don't think things to death. For heaven's sake –MAKE A DECISION.

Indecision—the third biggest enemy of success.

CHAPTER 81

EMBRACE YOUR FAILURES. THEY
ARE YOUR BEST TEACHER

I learned from early successes, but I learned much more from the things I did wrong and then changed. Some mistakes are very costly. If you can learn from the other guy's mistake, it sure beats making that mistake for yourself.

The gemstone business is a business that you can lose a year's profit in a single second. When I was just starting out, I had traveled over 4,000 miles on a buying trip. One of the stones I brought back was a fine Lightning Ridge black crystal opal. I spent several hours hand making a fine mounting for it with very sturdy prongs and proceeded to set the stone. I failed to slightly undercut the base of the prongs so that when the prongs were tightened around the stone, they bulged inward at the base and put enough pressure on the stone to break it. I was just starting out, and the mistake was devastating. It cost me thousands of dollars at a time when every single dollar was critical. It was a terrible blow. In the next thirty two years of my career, I didn't make that particular mistake again. Lesson learned!! Costly, but that mistake was certainly a good teacher.

I had paid $10,300 wholesale for a fine emerald. I made the wrong choice of which particular tool to use to set the stone. The result was a damaged emerald that lost most of its value. I had to sell the remaining much smaller, salvaged stone for $1,500 after I personally recut it. It was a net loss of $8,800 plus several hours of my re-cutting time.

The damage happened in a single second. I never made that mistake again. Lesson learned. Costly, but that mistake was certainly a good teacher.

On a real estate deal I had put down a $5,000 deposit on a contract for two parcels of waterfront land for $312,000. The balance of the down payment was due at closing, and I had arranged an owner financed payment schedule. One of the stipulations of the contract was that the owner was responsible for extending and connecting the municipal sewer before we went to closing.

We went to closing, and the seller hadn't completed the work to hook up the sewers as he had agreed, but the seller verbally promised to have it done within the month. If we cancelled the contract, which we should have done, we were afraid that we would never see our $5,000 deposit back, and we would lose the potential profit on the deal. The seller was not true to his word. To make a long story short, we later found that the seller had run afoul of the county inspector on some previous deals, and the inspector absolutely would not cooperate with him. TWO YEARS LATER, after dozens of phone calls and prodding to the seller, we found this out and went directly to the inspector ourselves and got the approval that very day. The problem was that the real estate market had tanked by then and we had lost all of the potential profit and actually took a very serious loss on the property. We lost over $122,000 because we weren't willing to cancel a contract. We would have only possibly lost $5,000 if we had followed our gut instinct and cancelled the closing. We never made that mistake again. Never, ever, close a deal before ALL of the terms are met. The other guy may have a different set of morals and rules than you do. When we give our word, we honored it. He didn't. Costly, but that mistake was certainly a good teacher.

It might be said that the only way to keep from making mistakes or failures is to just not do anything. Not so. If you do nothing, you will be nothing. Try and fail. Try again and do not repeat what you did wrong. You will eventually succeed. Embrace each failure as a big billboard that flashes in front of you that reminds you to not repeat the thing that didn't work.

You have heard of the "peanut gallery". It is that bleacher of people who are always around to taunt you and remind you of any failures you make. They delight secretly and sometimes even openly in your failures because it helps justify their own failures. I have found the best way to handle those people. Openly admit to the failure before they can point it out to you. It completely disarms their ridicule and rains on their party. Your own open admission of your mistake proves that you already learned the lesson from it, and they can't really fault that wisdom. They will sit there in silence and secretly admire you for being able to admit a mistake.

Embrace your failures. They are your best teacher.

CHAPTER 82

YOUR PRIDE CAN DESTROY YOU, AND IT ALSO KEEPS YOU FROM LEARNING

If you study the great religions of the world, one of the strongest common threads that interconnect their teachings is about pride. Essentially, spiritual enlightenment is only achieved after the individuals pride is reigned in and replaced by the realization that we are a small part of a whole, and our individuality is miniscule and insignificant. We find our "self" by losing our self-importance. We essentially lose our pride and sense of self-importance in subjugation to a greater order and power. That is the religious significance of pride, but there is even more.

When you are consumed with an inflated sense of self, you are unable to learn because in your mind, you really believe that you are superior to practically everyone around you. How could you possibly learn anything from anyone who you consider to be your inferior? You can never really be a student, so you go on with your delusion of superiority, but learn nothing. You keep telling yourself that you really are already superior to keep bolstering your inflated pride and ego. Your ultimate destruction will come soon enough because other people will stop wanting to deal with you.

In a third way, pride is destructive because it keeps you from ever putting yourself into a position where you might look foolish by making a mistake, so you just don't do anything to jeopardize your illusion of infallibility. You never take measured risks because you couldn't stand the blow to your ego and pride if you failed. Without measured risks you will achieve very little, and your life progress will slow to a crawl.

Your pride can destroy you, and also keeps you from learning.

CHAPTER 83

YOUR VIEW OF YOURSELF DEFINES YOUR POSITION IN LIFE

Psychiatrists and psychologists who were clients of our business agree that we tend to become what we are constantly told that we are. If you are constantly told that you are incompetent or stupid or unlikeable, sooner or later that image will permeate your psyche. On the other hand, if you are constantly told that you are intelligent and likeable, the likelihood of you actually being intelligent and likeable will increase. You can sabotage yourself by not believing in yourself and acting upon a positive view of yourself. Some kids grow up with a constant barrage of insults and degradation, and it generally reflects in their self-image and follows them until they realize that they alone are able to be whatever they decide to be.

If you view yourself positively and view yourself as the work in progress that we all are, you will see yourself as deserving of good things. You will tend to become a better person. You think of yourself as a good person on the way to becoming an even better person.

If you view yourself negatively and unable to change, your life will become more limited with less opportunities because you have convinced yourself that you are already lacking in whatever you have been told you were lacking. It will make you think that you really don't deserve success. It is extremely damaging and can follow you all through life unless you understand it and reverse it. The sooner, the better.

EVERYONE DESERVES SUCCESS. It is up to each of us to go after it. Don't allow comments from friends, parents, or anyone else deter you from holding onto your positive self-image. Listen to good council, but then capitalize on your good traits to reinforce a healthy self-image. Recognize where you need work and consistently work to improve those traits with the healthy realization that everyone can use some improvement. Don't focus and dwell on your weakest points without also recognizing your good traits. We are all a combination of weak and strong points. Just keep your perspective.

Your peak position in life will never be any higher than you have convinced yourself to be. If you only think you deserve a mediocre existence, then that is what you will have. Subconsciously, you will stop trying for a higher level of achievement because you don't think you really deserve more and you will sabotage your journey.

It doesn't matter what level of society you were born in financially. You are the master of your destiny if you will take the reins.

Your view of yourself defines your position in life.

CHAPTER 84

DISHONESTY WILL CATCH UP WITH YOU AND DESTROY YOUR SUCCESS

The newspapers are full of stories of highly accomplished and successful people that had forgotten one important rule along the way. Their success and reputation was destroyed because they did dishonest or illegal things. Crime actually does pay—until you are caught. Believe me you WILL be caught! The investigative tools of all law enforcement agencies are highly sophisticated in modern society. If you have done wrong and they focus on you, they WILL catch you.

You might go on for weeks, months or years, but eventually you WILL be caught and lose everything if you deal dishonestly. If the immorality of being dishonest doesn't deter you, then the certainty of being caught, ruined, losing everything, and serve years in prison should deter you.

Dishonest dealings will wreck your business quickly because people talk. Word of mouth can be the best thing you can have to build a business as long as you always deal fairly and honestly. It is devastating to a business as soon as you start to deal shady and dishonestly. Once the word is out that you are dishonest, it is impossible to regain a good reputation, and you will have to become a predator yourself to even survive. You will have to continually look for new people to cheat that have never heard about your dishonesty. That is like running from the law. It doesn't work.

How many politicians, businessmen, and religious leaders have lost their reputations, their fortunes, and their freedom by deciding to do some shady deal or engaged in immoral behavior? The list is long and sad.

The more successful you become financially, the more tempting it is to cheat on taxes. It is a common mistake that takes down a lot of people. Don't do it!!! You should study taxes and take every legal tax deduction you can, but don't break the law. The IRS is a seriously formidable enemy. If you ever get on their tax cheat list, you will be under their microscope from then on. You owe something to the great country that allows you to become successful with a flawed but workable system. Your taxes are absolutely necessary to pay for all of the conveniences of civilization such as roads, government services, and other infrastructure that you use and enjoy.

Honesty is the simplest path to sustained success. Dishonesty is a fool's realm. Dishonesty is a fast road up, but it is a freefall down.

Dishonesty will catch up with you and will destroy your success.

CHAPTER 85

A FILTHY MOUTH IS NOT ACCEPTABLE IN MOST BUSINESS SITUATIONS

I will admit to using some swear words sometimes in my private life and even a few filthy words from time to time as an expletive. I don't use them in business, and I don't use them as easy flowing sentence by sentence vernacular. Filthy language and swear words are offensive to many people. They denote a person who has no restraint and no manners. Yes, there are circles that use the "F" word in almost every sentence, but most people want to take a shower after they are around people like that. Nothing makes me cringe in disgust myself more than hearing a string of sentences with the "F" word craftily fitted everywhere it can possibly be inserted. Those words lose their punch if used too often or at the wrong time. When is the right time? Try "never" in any business situation, in mixed company, or with children around.

How many raving, swearing rants do you see on the national or local news? If a TV personality uses that kind of language on the air, they will be fired. In all the years I have done business in corporations, small businesses, and in businesses of my own, I have never heard strings of swear words used in daily conversations and business. Filthy language is simply a habit that is learned, and it can just as easily be unlearned. Regular casual use of filthy language diminishes your standing among most high caliber people. Rubbing shoulders with the right caliber of people will help cure that. Rubbing shoulders with the wrong kind of people will make you more prone to use filthy language.

It is like showing the worst side of yourself on a billboard that screams "I am uncouth, I have a limited vocabulary, and I constantly out of control. I am so frustrated that I only know how to express myself with basal terms and filthy words". Is that really the impression you want to project to the world?

If you are accustomed to using a string of filthy words, stop it and work on substituting words that will communicate meaning clearly and precisely. It is far more effective.

A filthy mouth is not acceptable in most business situations.

CHAPTER 86

SHARE YOUR KNOWLEDGE AS YOU PROGRESS. IT PAYS DIVIDENDS

When you become successful and it actually becomes a habit, you will realize that you couldn't have gotten there without learning from people who have gone before you. I have been mentored by many people, and I have been very grateful for each lesson they taught me from their own life experiences and business experiences. If humanity is ever going to really advance, one thing has to be conquered. People will have to listen and learn more from the people before them. Otherwise, each generation will continue to re-learn the same things over and over without much overall progress for mankind in general.

I will quote Benjamin Franklin once again. "Experience keeps a dear school, but a fool will learn in no other!" Try at every opportunity to pass on the positive things you learn with anyone who will listen. Sometimes a seed is planted that takes years to take root and grow. I always like to listen to older people and ask them about their experiences in their time. They grew up in a different world than I did, and by understanding what they experienced, I am able to shed light on things that are directly relevant to me. Our present culture idolizes youth. Looking young and acting young are almost a mantra in our culture. Age and experience are revered much more in most other cultures.

It is good to give your knowledge to the next generation by helping anyone you can. If you can make their path a little easier, you are helping all of humanity.

Share your knowledge as you progress. It pays dividends.

CHAPTER 87

DIFFICULTIES CREATE OPPORTUNITIES

The more common way to say this is "If the world gives you lemons, make lemonade!"

One of the best examples of this is the following true story.

I was fortunate enough to do significant business with a very famous diamond cutting firm in New York called Lazare Kaplan and Sons. They were world renown for their Ideal Cut Diamonds with mathematically precise cutting proportions that made the brightest and most scintillating finished diamonds. I was at their offices in a high rise building overlooking Central Park on one of my New York trips. As luck would have it, Lazare Kaplan, who was 92 years old at the time, was in the office that particular day. I had come out of one of the cutting rooms with Mr. Kaplan's son, George, who was in charge of the cutting operations for large and important diamonds. George had just shown me a diamond which was still on the cutting wheel that had started at over 23 carats as a raw crystal and had been on the cutting wheel for over six months. It had been a very difficult stone. It was now just over 9 carats, and they were putting the finishing touches on a top quality stone that was worth big bucks. It was particularly difficult to cut because it had internal knots and twinning lines in it. That is sort of like a tree with knots in it and had visible lines where two crystals had grown together. The grain of the diamond didn't run the same way throughout the crystal. The knots and twinning lines were causing significant problems because they don't polish evenly. It was a top grade stone, but a nearly impossible stone to finish because of the knots and twinning. They just kept cutting and cutting to remove the grain lines because it wouldn't polish correctly. Lazare was in the office that day to consult on the diamond because he was THE world expert on cutting diamonds with knots and grain lines. How did he get that reputation?

As a young diamond cutter, Lazare was unable to buy uncut diamonds direct from the mining consortium for two reasons. He was young and relatively inexperienced, and also, because his business was so small at the time, he couldn't afford to buy the quantity that the mining consortium required for direct purchase. Lazare had to buy any rough diamonds he could get from wherever he could get them. Problem diamonds from other dealers who didn't want to mess with them was all he could buy. The problem diamonds were all misshapen crystals that were inefficient to cut and knotted and twinned crystals that were very difficult to polish. Lazare took these difficult crystals that the other cutters didn't want. He used them to study any and all ways to make them commercially viable because that was all he could get. In short, it forced him to become the world's best cutter.

He didn't like it, but he made lemonade out of lemons. He persisted in developing methods to cut the problem stones and became known in the diamond business as a problem solver. Other dealers brought problem stones to him for consultation and for cutting. His reputation grew so large that the world renowned dealer Harry Winston came to him to consult on the uncut Jonker Diamond crystal which weighed 726 carats. At the time it was the fourth largest diamond that had ever been found. It had been studied by several other expert diamond cutters for months before Lazare was called in to study it. The other cutters had agreed to cut it a particular direction. After studying it for many weeks more, Lazare decided that if the stone was cut as planned by the other cutters, it would have been "off grain" when the stone was cleaved (split) for further cutting into precisely efficient stones. It would end up in the stone being shattered or badly damaged. Harry Winston listened to Lazare because of Lazare's experience with problem diamonds and decided after careful consideration to entrust the cutting to him. If a diamond is cleaved even a tiny amount off grain it can shatter. With great trepidation, Lazare very carefully struck the cleaving blow to the crystal with a wedged steel cleaving knife and hammer. The stakes couldn't be higher. Several million of today's dollars were riding on that single precise hammer blow on the cleaver wedge. It cleaved perfectly into two parts with no waste exactly as Lazare had planned after long and careful study. The news went out all over the world and Lazare became world famous.

Lazare's other son Leo, who was the CEO of the Corporation, first introduced me to his father Lazare. I smiled and shook hands with a fully erect man six feet tall with a neat handlebar moustache and perfect posture. He was bright, cordial and alert. I was star struck by the 92 year old legend. The most famous diamond cutter in the world was shaking my hand! In my usual curious manner, I asked him about his role in developing the ideal cut with his cousin Marcel Tolkowski. Evidently, nobody had asked about that in many years, and he seemed delighted that I would be interested. I was transfixed by his story of how he had done the experimental cutting for his cousin to study the effects of angles and proportions on diamond brilliance. Tolkowski had written "Diamond Design" which was actually his college thesis on the mathematical angle studies for diamond proportions. As Lazare was talking to me, I didn't want to break eye contact with him, but George had slipped around behind me and turned my hand over and put something in it. I wanted to give my full attention to the legend before me, so I didn't look at what George had slipped into my hand but I imagined what it was.

That very day, the traveling exhibit of the largest uncut diamond in the world had come back into the Kaplan office for recertification and inspection. At an appropriate moment after Lazare had finished his story, I glanced down at my hand. In my hand rested an uncut diamond crystal weighing over 610 carats that George had just put there. I was holding the world's largest uncut diamond at that time in my hand, and I was talking to the greatest legend in the diamond business at the same time! If my grandkids are interested, I will tell them personally about the famous natural colored diamond collection I also held that day in my hands. It is one of the most famous natural colored diamond collections in the world.

Another example of a person using difficulties to create opportunities was Frank. Frank was a very colorful and very handsome Cuban businessman who was a client in our gem business. He had striking wavy white hair and a casual smile with heavy eyebrows to match the white hair. I admired him because he espoused many of the things I had found to be true in doing business, but he was about 30 years my senior. He was as tight and frugal as me, and I respected how he did business. He also knew how to make lemonade out of lemons.

One day he told me one of his many business secrets. There are very small and oddly shaped pieces of land that are literally useless in all cities. They are too small to build on, too small to get permits to do anything with—except—the huge signs you see all up and down the streets and highways of any town or city. Frank would check the county records (long before the internet made it so easy) to find out who owned the slivers of odd shaped tiny pieces of land. He would find out where they lived and go to their house and make cash offers to the people to buy them. The owners were paying continual taxes on the useless pieces and were generally glad to get rid of them for a few hundred dollars. Frank would then go to a sign construction company and erect huge steel lighted signs on them for a few thousand dollars. He would then rent the advertising space for up to $1,200 a month for each side! These are the kind of signs that line all major highways. The land and signs would pay for themselves in a few short months. It was mostly profit after that. The money rolled in indefinitely! That is some pretty profitable lemons!

When my wife and I looked for real estate to purchase, we always looked for the problems and for the potentials that other people overlooked. Most people are lazy, and they don't want to get into anything that is difficult. Most people don't have imagination and can't see the potential of a piece of property.

Apply imaginative thinking to all situations, and see if you can turn your lemons into lemonade.

Difficulties create opportunities.

CHAPTER 88

THE FIRST STEP IS THE HARDEST TO MAKE BECAUSE YOU HAVE TO OVERCOME THE FEAR OF EMBARRESSMENT

None of want to be embarrassed. The fear of being embarrassed is so strong that some people would rather live their lives playing it safe and be a failure or be mediocre. Some people's ego is so inflated that they think that they can never allow themselves to appear that they could make a mistake. Their egos are so fragile, and their true inner self confidence is so low that they just can't bear the risk of looking like they aren't in full control of every situation. They have a deep seated need to always appear to be right. An inflated ego is deadly to your success. Pride is also deadly to your success. Every person who has attained any degree of success has a long string of false starts and failures. They don't dwell on them. They don't let the failures define their lives. They learn from failures, correct the defect in their actions, and go forward by taking the first step again and again until they get it right. Each time they mess up and embarrass themselves it is painful, but they have learned that the pain and embarrassment is a vital part of learning. It is so emotionally painful that they have the incentive to not repeat that particular mistake again. They are only defeated if they don't continue to take that hardest step—the first one. The worst embarrassment is to never take that first step, never try, and surely fail because you defeated yourself with inaction.

The first step is the hardest to make because you have to overcome your fear of embarrassment.

CHAPTER 89

DO THINGS THAT YOU REALLY BELIEVE IN.

There is big money in many things that I don't believe in. I won't invest in them, and I won't do business in any of them because of my code of beliefs. The code I subscribe to isn't particularly religious, but instead it is practical. You can't oppose something and be enthusiastic to make money from it either by investing in the product or investing in the stocks of the business itself. The potential profits don't matter. You have to stand for something in life and be true to your beliefs.

There is big money in oil and coal, but I don't believe in them or invest in them because of the damage to our environment. I believe we already have the technology to succeed them and make the need for them obsolete, but the corrupt system won't allow it out into the marketplace. I believe there is a better way.

There is big money in marijuana and other reality altering drugs. I don't believe in them and won't invest in them even if they become legal because of the damage they cause in people's lives and to the nation.

There is big money in booze and alcohol. I don't believe in it and won't invest in it because of the first hand destruction it has caused to my father and millions of others.

There is big money in tobacco and more recently in vaping, I don't believe in it and I won't invest in it because smoking killed my mother and millions of others.

There is big money in nuclear energy. I don't believe in it because the storage and deactivation of radioactive waste that is toxic for tens of thousands of years is a time bomb. That hasn't been solved and unlikely will be in the near future.

I don't believe in products that are designed to self-destruct or wear out so quickly that they are a poor value. They are a drain on our natural resources.

There is huge money in "creative" financial services and banking. The way most of them are practiced today, I won't have anything to do with them because they are designed to fleece the investor.

I would rather make far less money on something I truly believe in than to get wealthy on something that I don't believe in.

Enthusiasm is a key factor in making anything a success, and if you can't have enthusiasm for what you do in life, you shouldn't be doing it. Enthusiasm is infectious. In and of itself, enthusiasm is the driving force behind success.

In the decision making processes I outlined in Chapter 80 and other chapters, I have given you an exercise in deductive reasoning. The decision possibilities are narrowed down to a fewer number with each step. Soon, the final answer becomes obvious. Use deductive reasoning in your career and investment choices, and form your future around the things that you believe in. If you are fascinated by constructing things, maybe something to do with the construction will give you the most satisfaction. Maybe you love creating beauty, and something to do with art or architecture would be right for you. Whatever it is, find your passion, and go for it!

One of my passions was the fascination with rare and valuable things, so I made three of my businesses related to gemstones, jewelry, and precious metals like gold, silver, platinum, and palladium, and to art in several forms. I just love handling the stuff. I love its inherent beauty and believe in it as a financial instrument. Rare and beautiful things are a good place to store value. You need to feel the same enthusiasm for what you decide to do. I also believe in the long lasting value of real estate and land. I get excited when I think about all of the possibilities of how each particular land parcel or house could be changed to be more valuable and usable. That is called "converting to a higher usage", and it is a basic strategy in real estate. It is almost like printing money.

Do things that you really believe in.

CHAPTER 90

THINK OUT OF THE BOX.

My wife and I have always been "out of the box thinkers". My wife has a saying that we have both lived our lives by. She is very challenging and doesn't take the garbage that people like to throw around like "It is our policy!" Her answer is "Says who"!!!? She doesn't respond if something doesn't make complete sense to her. You are a fool if you try to approach her with a half-baked thought because she will make mincemeat of you. That is one of the many reasons I married her.

Question and challenge everything until it makes sense to you. The most successful people throughout history and in the future are those that are somewhat contrarian in their view of the world. Don't blindly accept anything until you are truly convinced of its truth. That goes for religion, for politics, or for facts in a physics book. The so called "laws" of physics are merely constructs of man to help explain what he has the intelligence to perceive at any given point in time. Those laws change as we learn more.

One of my favorite sayings is attributed to Arthur Schopenhauer (1788-1860). He said "The truth passes through three stages:

First– it is ridiculed.

Second– it is violently opposed.

Third– it is accepted as self-evident.

I keep this saying taped onto on the side of my computer at all times.

All new ways of doing things, and all inventions go through these three steps.

In order to be on the front edge of anything, you have to see a truth before others do. You have to maintain the courage of your convictions to buck the world to give birth to any new innovation. Believe in yourself enough to trust your judgment more as you mature in your success. Don't be afraid to insist on understanding anything completely. Most people are full of baloney and talk a lot about things that they really don't know much about. The advantage of hanging around successful people is that they usually DO know what they are talking about because they are "doers" and not just "talkers". Develop your skills at differentiating the "talkers and wishers" from the "doers". People respect others that insist on getting the facts straight even though they are challenged and intimidated by them. They are definitely inconvenient to deal with. Insisting on understanding everything that is told to you intimidates people who are trying to "snow" you, but it draws people of substance to you because you are like them. They understand you.

Try to look at the world from many different viewpoints and attack every problem with wide open parameters. Use deductive reasoning to narrow the possibilities down to fewer and fewer until the answer becomes more evident.

Out of the box thinkers are "brainstormers" who come up with seemingly ridiculous ideas — at first. I was an industrial technician for a couple of years in a cable factory, and I was a technician in the research department of a lens manufacturing plant at another time. In both positions, my ideas and experiments on industrial processes were incorporated into manufacturing processes. I came up with both processes by out of the box thinking. As is customary, any process I came up with belonged to the corporation because I had signed a forfeiture agreement when I was hired. One idea was a contrarian designed feed screw for a plastic extruder that was used to manufacture high frequency coaxial communications cable. The other process was a revolutionary and impossible process for polishing bifocal segments into eyeglass lens molds that everyone told me was impossible until I proved them wrong. I just employed my knowledge of cutting and polishing gemstones to cutting and polishing glass. I was initially ridiculed and told that what I was doing wouldn't work by men who were limited by their formal education. They were establishment thinkers and not out of the box thinkers. None of them had ever polished gemstones. Don't challenge an out of the box thinker because he will likely prove to you that a completely different approach to a problem will solve the problem. The blinders of a more normal approach keep others from seeing some obscure detail that you perceive if you think out of the box.

One of the biggest secrets to success in real estate is being able to visualize a higher usage for the land or buildings, or to visualizing changes to them that would make them more desirable and marketable. The more creative you teach yourself to be, the more innovations you manifest. Re-read about Frank in Chapter 87.

Think out of the box.

CHAPTER 91

KEEP CHANGING YOUR "ASSEMBLAGE POINT" TO SEE NEW PERSPECTIVES.

This chapter is actually more advanced than other chapters, and it is meant more for you after you are already pretty adept at thinking out of the box with some successes under your belt. I don't expect you to completely understand the concept I am about to introduce you to, but mentally file it away for when you are ready for it.

A person's "assemblage point" is the position in the world from which they view all things. It is more than the physical location. It is more than a time frame. It is more than a temporary mindset. It is more than an educational level. It is more than a religious or moral structure. It is more than a cultural point of view. It is more than an empathetic understanding of others. It is more than the patriotic view toward your country. It is more than the allegiance to your friends or family.

"ASSEMBLAGE POINT" is the essence of your entire self and how you relate to all things. It is much more philosophical than merely a "viewpoint". It is more of a "being point".

In order to always be able to perceive completely different and new concepts and unrealized possibilities, you have to challenge your assemblage point to see things from a combination of perspectives that nobody else has ever consciously seen them before. It is the next step higher than just thinking out of the box. It is the realm of great thinkers. This will seem pretty mystical to you right now, but I am outlining the mental state where really novel and completely untried ideas are born. I am merely mentioning it here because it is the extension to thinking out of the box which was discussed in the last chapter.

This is not the level you will be ready to work in until you are fluent in thinking out of the box in every pursuit. This is the realm of really marvelous and world changing ideas that literally leave most people in the dust. If you are frustrated by constant conversational dribble, shallow thinking, and the ineptitude of many people, you might have the mindset to consider continually altering your assemblage point. Maybe you have what it takes to come up with some really revolutionary approach to a product or process. Most of the world does not operate at this level, and if you do, you will need great conviction to survive the opposition and ridicule.

A good example of changing your assemblage point is to challenge a problem as if you were seeing it for the first time from any and all perspectives. See it from any possible perspective that looks concealed from the typical observer. I changed my assemblage point when I realized at age 50 that the world actually operates much different than I had always thought. I saw the world from a poor person's point of view, a rich person's point of view, a religious person's point of view, a scientist's point of view, a criminal's point of view, and a philanthropist's point of view. Each person has his/her own perceived reality that is what they perceive as reality which is subjective. Each interpretation of reality varies with mindset.

Look at the problem from the point of view of someone who has no money whatsoever, is old, is young, or is in any way different than you.

Learn to figuratively climb inside the skin of another being (including animals, plants, and inanimate objects) with different attributes than yourself to detect that invisible thing that is missed by everyone else. Sounds pretty far out doesn't it?

Look at it from the point of view of someone who has a completely different religious point of view and political point of view than you.

Look at it from completely unreasonable and unrealistic ways by employing what is called "possibility thinking". Research scientists as opposed to practical scientists must do this regularly. They create hypotheses and invent things before there is a need and then they, or someone else, find a need afterwards.

Look specifically where a detail could have been overlooked by everyone else.

Consider new and different materials or new and different applications of materials.

It is what detectives do to solve crimes. They climb into the skin of the perpetrator and think like the perpetrator thinks. They change their assemblage point by thinking in a completely different way.

I know this seems kind of mystical. It really isn't. If you don't understand it, don't worry. It is advanced and difficult for most people to grasp until it happens to you, but out of the box thinkers get it at some point.

Keep changing your "assemblage point" to see new perspectives.

CHAPTER 92

DON'T GET TOO LOFTY AND LOSE YOUR HUMANITY AS YOU GET RICH

If you follow and use the information in this book, you WILL get rich. There is absolutely no doubt about it. It is not even the faintest chance that you will not get rich IF you faithfully do what I have outlined for you to do in this book. I hope you are working on many other successes along with financial successes, too, because money alone is a hollow victory.

With money comes responsibility. You had to accept full responsibility for your actions to become rich, and now the next immediate task is to stay rich. How do you do that?

If you start acting irresponsibly and spend to your income limit, you will very soon become poor again. If you succumb to all of the people around you, including friends and family, who want what you have earned, but aren't willing to listen to you to help themselves to attain it, you will ride their guilt train back into poverty. There is no end to the people who think you should just give them some money. The more they think you have, the more they want. Those people won't listen to you when you tell them how to manage better and make their own money to make their own lives better. They think you should just give them some of yours.

This parable is pretty accurate. "Give a man a fish, and you will feed him for a day. Teach him how to fish, and you will feed him for a lifetime".

This book is the equivalent of teaching you how to fish, financially.

When you are wealthy and successful in other ways, you have a responsibility to make sure that your own life remains strong so in a real crisis you can help family members or others. You can only help them if you remain strong financially yourself.

People whine and flail around as soon as they become uncomfortable, but if they are left alone, they will figure out a way to get through most things they consider crises, but aren't. Invariably, their problems are caused by their poor management, poor decisions, or just plain laziness. In the event of a true crisis, I will step in and do what is necessary.

I have provided for all of my family in the event of a true crisis, but I allow them to flail around with the minor incidents to allow them to build their own ingenuity. Some people never learn. Some do.

Never get the idea that you are somehow an elite person when you acquire money. You are just a person who has learned financial skills to make your life better and you developed the discipline to do it. Be free with your new knowledge, but be prepared: VERY FEW PEOPLE WHO HEAR INFORMATION REQUIRING THEM TO GET OFF THEIR BUTTS WILL ACTUALLY DO WHAT YOU ADVISE THEM TO DO. Many people are just plain lazy.

Many people won't believe that it is so easy to become wealthy. Many other people will think that the self-discipline and delayed gratification are just too hard, and they won't do it.

Don't become just another jackass with money. Don't flaunt your money by foolish and lavish living. First of all, it is dangerous and makes you a target for thieves, con artists, leeches, greedy and lazy friends, family, and frivolous lawsuits. Secondly, it leads to a scenario where you will have to keep up an image of wealth. You will become a slave to the false prestige of a new car, the fancy clothes, the expensive house, and the country club memberships. Live quietly and allow people to think that you are poorer than you really are. You have nothing to prove. If all of those entrapments are what you really want, I can't help you further. I'll see you on the way down and back into poverty.

Don't get too lofty and lose your humanity as you get rich.

CHAPTER 93

AT SOME POINT YOUR BIGGEST PROBLEM WILL BE WHERE TO PUT ALL OF THE MONEY TO WORK (IT'S HARD TO BELIEVE, BUT IT IS TRUE)

I was told early in my career that the most difficult problem was going to be to decide where to put all of the money that started to flow in. Only a very few years later, that did become one of my biggest problems and continues to be.

I know it sounds ridiculous to someone who works for a few dollars per hour and exists from paycheck to paycheck that they could have so much money flowing in that they wouldn't know what to do with it. I assure you that if you do exactly what I am telling you to do in this book, keeping your money working prudently will become a serious issue for you.

To people unskilled in finances, spending money for instant gratification of all desires is the first thing that comes to mind. As soon as they start to accumulate a little money, they start eating high with expensive foods and meals in restaurants until the foods that were once special become commonplace. They start buying expensive clothing until they realize that expensive designer clothing for most things is a waste of money. They live lavishly to show off their newfound wealth by buying a new car, a big house, and generally display their wealth. They get socially entrapped into the lavish lifestyle that is very difficult to retreat from. They will do anything to avoid looking like a diminishing fool who is already on the way back down to poverty or, heaven forbid, "a loser". Then they become a slave to the lavish lifestyle just as they were a slave to their paycheck before they became wealthy. That is the mentality of the poor expressed by someone who temporarily has money but didn't learn the vital lessons of money. They won't have it for long.

I'm not saying that you shouldn't enjoy the fruits of your labor. It is o.k. to eat a nice meal out sometimes, to drive a near new car within your budget if you have the cash to pay for it, to own a few articles of fine clothing, and spend a budgeted amount of money on entertainment. Just do it in moderation and not as a lifestyle to impress others. Always keep in mind that the nice things are only special if they don't become commonplace to you.

The nearer you come to becoming a sustained millionaire, the less you actually even want to spend. It is almost like the kid in the candy store that eats candy until he is sick. You will know that you have matured into wealth when you are automatically careful with every dollar you have, and actually don't like to spend money anymore. Spending is almost the opposite of investing. Every dollar spent is a dollar that is consumed and not available to invest.

Instead of putting your time into how fast you can spend your million, put the time into how to keep that million, and make it grow perpetually with passive income.

The world will present you with numerous places to invest, but most of them are just a fantasy or a con job. Continually improve your ability to carefully analyze any situation for possible pitfalls, and set up a very strict standard that you require before you invest any money. Be a tough sell in all of your business dealings.

At some point your biggest problem will be where to put all of the money to work (It's hard to believe, but it is true!)

CHAPTER 94

DELAYED GRATIFICATION IS ESSENTIAL FOR SUCCESS. THE NEED FOR INSTANT GRATIFICATION BREEDS POVERTY

Some chapters are so important that I can nearly guarantee that you will fail at life and fail at financial success, if you don't apply them.

THIS IS ONE OF THOSE CRITICALLY IMPORTANT CHAPTERS!

It is one of the most important lessons in this book.

Delayed gratification is the ability to be disciplined enough to stay on course toward your goal, any goal, until you complete it.

ALL PEOPLE WHO ARE SUCCESSFUL ARE SKILLED AT SAYING "NO" TO ANYTHING THAT DISTRACTS THEM FROM THEIR GOALS. They finish what they start. They know that nothing worthwhile comes without consistent effort.

If you are the kind of person that always finishes the things you start, then you are already aware of how important delayed gratification is. If you have homework for a course, you do it before you do other things that are momentarily more fun. If someone tries to get you to go out and have fun, your answer is "Sorry, I have to study. Maybe later". You know that studying will help you get to your long term goal of graduating, so you set the proper priorities for your future and don't let the feeling of the moment govern your future. You don't give in to your weaknesses. You don't find it necessary to spend several dollars per day to "treat" yourself. You are not a trivial reward junkie requiring a constant "fix". You realize that the real reward will come by delaying your gratification long enough to make real progress.

If you are the kind of person that has to impulsively buy things you see to feel good for the moment, you need some serious work at controlling your urges and wants. You have indulged yourself to expect instant satisfaction at the price of real improvement of your future. You are probably living a pretty dull and uninteresting life that has a limited future. You have to feel instant gratification every day in order to get through life. You are addicted to a "quick fix".

Think carefully about getting involved with any pursuit. Determine that it is really something worth going for, and then DO it. Commit to it wholeheartedly and use delayed gratification to fend off the need for instant satisfaction to make you "feel good" at every turn. FINISH WHAT YOU START, AND DON'T START THINGS THAT YOU WON'T FINISH. Take your satisfaction when the big goals are completed after a long pursuit. If you commit to a college degree, then don't let any obstacle stop you. If you decide to start a business, go all in and make it happen. Don't allow your laziness, your vices, your bad habits, or your need to continually spoil yourself with minor rewards slow or stop your progress.

I'm sure you know people that allow video games, cliques of friends, entertainment, cars, clothes, sex, laziness, alcohol, drugs, reward food, excess sleeping, or just hanging out, consume their time and money so they never seem to be able to advance to a higher level. Excess interest in all of these things is a sure sign of someone who is destined for a mundane existence because they have to constantly be rewarding themselves with instant gratification. They live life in the short term and don't plan for the long term.

The person who can look to the future and keep it in perspective while also living in the present will have few regrets as they pass through life. Just don't sacrifice your future wellbeing and financial stability by consuming all your resources on daily pleasures and habits. If you feed your daily pleasures and habits at the expense of your financial investments, you will slow or stop your financial progress, and you will never become wealthy. Remember that becoming wealthy will make it much easier to attain all of your other goals.

Delayed gratification is essential for financial success. The need for instant gratification breeds poverty.

CHAPTER 95

THINK LIKE AN ENTREPRENEUR AND A BOSS. DON'T HAVE AN EMPLOYEE MINDSET

It has taken me many years to accept that there are some people who just have an employee mindset. They don't have enough drive and sense of adventure to lead. They have to fit into an organization and follow the direction of someone else. They find comfort in being like the people around them and fitting in.

There is definitely a difference between an employer's mindset and an employee's mindset. The employer has to think up what to do next, and the employee waits to be told what to do next. Many people simply don't want or can't handle the responsibility of self-starting and self-determination.

Corporations and large organizations are a very good place for people with an employee mindset because they can find their place somewhere in the pecking order and feel comfortable. At the very top of all organizations is the man (or woman) on the white horse. They are the thinker, the doer, the innovator. If they don't do it themselves, they are smart enough to find the people who will function in every station below them to accomplish it. They are the boss. They have an employer mindset. They make the big bucks because they are skilled in decision making and are skilled in finding others with a lesser degree of a boss's mindset than they have themselves. All of the people below the boss who function at lesser levels, have consecutively lesser levels of a boss mindset and more of an employee mindset. Our educational system is designed to provide those people to the economy. Every person at the top has had to learn many of the things in this book to get where they are. Frankly, most people don't want the responsibility of being the boss. They want their free weekends, 40 hour week, a predictable schedule, and benefits. That's o.k. if that is what you want. That won't get you the independence of self-determination or the freedom of financial security unless you also follow the frugal practices in this book. You must wisely invest a significant portion of EVERY DOLLAR you make over a very long time.

If you like working in a corporation, that's fine, but don't just become a cog in a wheel. Have your financial future separated from your corporate activities, and be simultaneously be running your personal financial life separately as a business.

An entrepreneur will ask, "What precise steps can I take to start this business and make it continually profitable?" He considers rent, capital, professional expertise, labor and employees, licenses, insurance, security, minor expenses, inventory, suppliers, advertising, customer base, bookkeeping, banking, and any other unplanned circumstances. If you want to be an entrepreneur, you should be asking these questions. You won't concern yourself about wages because you know the sky is the limit if you perform. Any good boss will also be asking the same questions. The questions are about building and maintaining a business with long term goals in mind. As an entrepreneur, he will keep all of the profits, or as a boss he will keep a percentage of the profits in some form. He won't ask about work schedule because he knows that he will work long, long hours.

A person with an employee mindset will ask "How much vacation time do I get, what benefits do I get, how much do I get paid per hour or month, what is my work schedule, and how much sick leave do I get? They are all legitimate questions. At some time or other, I have been concerned about every one of them when I was young, short sighted, and had an employee mentality. All of the goals are immediate or near term goals designed to allow a predictable, and comfortable life. Employees typically are not directly concerned at all about how to make the corporation profitable enough to be able to make their paycheck. Employees sell their time. Time is limited, and the hours you have to sell are limited. The problem is, with an employee mentality, you will never progress past everyone else around you. In ten years, it is likely that you will be about where you are now with a few token raises that may not even match inflation. This is what most people settle for in life.

If you want to be a follower with a J.O.B. (JUST OVER BROKE), keep an employee mindset.

If you want to be financially free and make your own decisions, develop an entrepreneurial mindset or a boss's mindset.

Think like an entrepreneur and a boss. Don't have an employee mindset.

As a side note: Some businesses just require an idea and guts.

When I was fourteen years old, I started a business along with two other youngsters of sixteen and seventeen years. We were all into model rockets, and we were on a flight test crew for a small company called Model Missiles Incorporated. We had all won an invitation to attend the first World Congress of Flight in Las Vegas, Nevada to give a demonstration of model rocketry. Our demonstration was to be among all of the military hardware in a nationally televised air show. The show was to demonstrate the latest military and commercial aviation hardware from all over the world. We were given an all-expense paid trip including airfare. We were the youngest delegates to attend the United Nations dinner in Las Vegas. The next day, we met and talked to the 92 year old General Lamm (who flew with the Wright Brothers), and talked personally with the famous test pilot, Scott Crossfield, who flew the bell X-15 into the edge of space before the space program and NASA was started.

We contracted to build the rocket airframes for sales demonstrations throughout the country. The three of us kids formed the company we unabashedly called "Galactic Enterprises", with fatherly direction from the engineer, businessman and author G. Harry Stein who owned Model Missiles Inc. We thought the name sounded cool, but looking back on it, the name was a little optimistic. We also worked with a genius named Vern Estes who designed and built a marvelous automated machine to make model rocket engines that eventually became the famed Estes Enterprises which is still in operation today. We test flew some of his first engines. I was responsible for making the production jigs to assemble the airframes and to assemble them along with my slightly older friends. WE RAN THE BUSINESS IN A BASEMENT OUT OF SCRAP PARTS AND NO MONEY. We had a notarized legal written contract to produce 1500 rockets. For the summer, I earned more money at age fourteen than my father was making as a police detective. He responded to my first paycheck by congratulating me and started charging me rent at age fourteen! At the time I thought it was highly unfair, but it was one of the best lessons I ever learned. The contract resulted in a further commitment to develop a larger weather rocket which is another story. That airframe was similar in size and design to the famous military air to air heat seeking missile called "Sidewinder".

CHAPTER 96

GO DOWN THE STREET AND NOTICE ALL OF THE BUSINESSES. SOMEBODY OWNS EACH ONE. EXACTLY WHAT DID THEY DO TO GET THERE?

If you drive down any commercial street, you will see a wide diversity of businesses requiring very different specialized skills.

Some person has come up with the idea to start every single one of them and has studied through a list of things required to make their idea a reality. They first conceived an idea from a desire to create a business. Then, they investigated traffic flow and demographics, business licenses and permits, financing and banking, insurance, rent, labor, expert skills, fixtures, tools, showcases, office equipment, incidental costs, operational costs, accounting, advertising, marketing, signage, and parking, in order to come up with a business plan. Every single business you see had to address every single one of these factors. If they have been running for an extended time, every single one of them is making a very good living for someone or group of people if the business is being managed well.

Most modest startup businesses are much simpler to create and run than this list implies. This list is a more formal list for a business requiring a commercial business location in a bricks and mortar space. Today, many to most businesses are started in someone's spare room or garage. You are probably familiar with some of them. (Microsoft, Apple, Facebook). Let's not forget Galactic Enterprises. Just checking to see if you really read the whole book. I highly recommend starting in a garage or a bedroom. You have very low overhead and full control right under your fingertips! I started several businesses like that. Your first business should be one that is simple. Just be logical and thorough. Look carefully before you leap.

A person might feel like they are missing out on the "American Dream" if they don't own and run at least one business. They are!

The exact kind of business doesn't matter. Almost any business can make big money if it is run properly. A grocery store can be just as profitable as a car dealership, a bowling alley, a hobby shop, a landscaping company, a real estate company, a trucking company, an internet company, or an art gallery. Each business has its strong points and drawbacks. Each business requires a particular set of skills unique to the business. All of them require certain personal people skills and business skills that are very similar no matter what product or service the business deals in. Once a person learns those basic business and people skills, they are applicable to all business. The problem is, those skills are not taught in school. They are acquired from working with people and doing business in the real world. A business degree is an o.k. place to start, but certainly not necessary unless you plan to go work for wages. The whole point of this book is to teach you how to NOT just work for wages.

I will actually prefer a person with years of personal skills derived from dealing in the real world with people any day over a person with a classroom degree in business.

All throughout my life I noticed that it was the business owners that lived better and freer than anyone I knew who worked for a salary or hourly wages. The business owners all worked just as hard or harder, but they also had far greater rewards and had the ability to be more flexible to handle emergencies and nice vacations than wage earners had. They all seemed to be in charge of their lives instead of being owned by a company. They were in charge of their own destiny. In our businesses, we closed every year for the entire month of August and went on international trips or family vacations because August was traditionally our slowest month. Some of our international buying trips were taken then.

Go down the street and notice all of the businesses. Somebody owns each one. Exactly what did they do to get there?

CHAPTER 97

WHEN SOMEBODY TELLS YOU "IT'S TOO COMPLICATED FOR YOU TO UNDERSTAND!" THEY ARE TRYING TO SNOW YOU.

The sure sign someone is trying to take advantage of you or to overwhelm you with illogical nonsense is when they tell you that "it is too complicated" and infer that you either don't have the mental capacity to understand or that they are so far superior to you that you couldn't possibly understand.

I have never been confronted by anything that I couldn't reason through or study enough to make some sense of it.

Any time someone tells you that "it is too complicated" to understand, insist that they back up and explain it in detail to you. You will soon expose them for what they are—charlatans. Crooked people use this phrase often to put you on the defensive and attempt to get you to accept their line of baloney. They know that most people won't defend themselves vigorously and challenge a confidence man (con artist). They want something from you, and the only way they can get it is to confuse you and intimidate you. Pseudo academics, pseudo religious leaders, politicians, and pseudo financial consultants are particularly prone to using this technique.

One of the best examples is the one I gave about the Senate hearings on the financial bailouts of 2008 which I described in CHAPTER 13 on inflation. Three pompous academics and bureaucrats (Gaither, Paulson, and Bernanke) snowed enough of the Senate to con them into voting for an enormous financial bailout of the banking system. Over and over they inferred, and also stated plainly, that the Senators couldn't possibly understand the intricacies of the financial system like they, themselves could. It amounted to one of the biggest robberies of the American taxpayer in history. Only a couple of Senators, including Betty Captor, saw through the baloney and trusted their own judgment to call it the fraud that it was. Most of the Senators were unwilling to forcibly ask the right questions to expose the fraud for fear of looking stupid. They were bullied into believing that they would destroy the financial base of the country if they didn't do exactly as they were being told—and do it NOW—without thinking about it. The insistence that the decision must be made instantly without due deliberation is another red flag. One by one, I watched Senators cower away from meaty questions as they interviewed these three characters. Always remember this: The only stupid question is the one that is not asked. One by one, Senators cowered away from getting to the real truth by being intimidated and fearful of looking like a fool on the Senate floor.

Never allow anyone to tell you that you couldn't possibly understand what they are saying. Make them educate you so you WILL understand. Never, never trust anyone who can't or won't take the time to explain their statement in detail so you WILL understand. Have the self-conviction to MAKE THEM JUSTIFY THEIR STATEMENTS.

When somebody tells you "It's too complicated for you to understand!" They are trying to snow you.

CHAPTER 98

MOST MILLIONAIRES DON'T LIVE LAVISHLY BECAUSE IT ISN'T SMART FINANCIALLY

An interesting thing happens as you build your financial wealth. You begin to respect money more and realize that its power is in using it wisely, and its power is in its potential. Having it is powerful. Investing it is powerful. Spending it is NOT powerful! You realize how easily money that is spent slips away in little bits at a time almost unnoticed. That is exactly what happens when you live lavishly. Your financial fortune is like a bucket full of water which has a tiny pinhole in it. The water leaks out so gradually that you only notice the leak after the water level has gone down significantly. A significant portion of your fortune will disappear, and you will wonder where it went.

If you have learned the lessons in previous chapters about keeping careful track of every penny you spend, and to invest most of your money rather than spend it. You will already be aware of how delicate it is to maintain a financial balance in your life. Treating yourself to some of your wants is fine AFTER you can afford it when you have excess money above your investments. At that point the money becomes self-sustaining due to passive investments.

I can't imagine that anyone who has really been poor would ever want to repeat that condition, but the quickest way to return to poverty is to live lavishly. Living openly lavishly might be a temporary boost to your ego, but is unsustainable and isn't wise financially.

If you show your wealth, you will become a target for confidence scams, robbers, and lawsuits. There are several levels of envious tax authorities who sometimes use arbitrarily worded laws to take away some of your money unfairly. Everyone wants to share in your success without working for it. If they are in doubt about your financial strength, they don't have a target to focus on. If you drive a flashy high performance sports car, you are much more likely to be harassed by traffic cops than if you drive a conservative car. If you get bids on anything from construction projects to car repairs, you are more likely to be charged more because you look like you can pay more. It isn't fair, but that is reality. It is better to appear as if you are really stretching to be able to afford something rather than trying to make a big splash and act pompous and wealthy. Only billionaires can get away with that. Millionaires are comfortably wealthy, but not stupid wealthy.

Most millionaires don't live lavishly because it isn't smart financially.

CHAPTER 99

DEVELOP AT LEAST ONE HIGH INCOME SKILL

Since the road to wealth requires seed money anyway, it is easier and quicker to earn that difficult seed money with a highly paid skill rather than working at or near minimum wages. Minimum wage works too, but it is more difficult and takes longer.

There are numerous skills that pay very well, but they all take time and dedication to master.

You can do it with knowledge in any field that is in demand. Electricians, carpenters, welders, instructors of anything, jewelers, traders in most products of high value, skilled repairmen, artists, performers, attorneys, medical technicians, people with really good computer skills, and inventors are just a few examples. Virtually anything that requires a skill that most other people don't have is a viable choice.

The things that are not as useful as a high income skill are what I call "drone" jobs that can be done by about anybody with little or no skill. Those jobs would include grocery cashiers, hamburger flippers, retail shelf stockers, pizza delivery drivers, janitorial workers, construction helpers, and laborers. I have personally done most of these and more in my early years, and they are all honorable, but they are a very temporary means to an end and don't qualify as high income skills. It has been said that all men are worth about the same amount of money from the neck down. The implication is that the important part which is worth the high pay comes from what is in the man from the neck up—knowledge and skill. The more rare and difficult the skill, generally the more valuable the person is.

Two of the skills that I learned over many years of education and practice that were highly paid were gemological appraising of gems and jewelry, and constructing expensive platinum jewelry. I charged as much as $1000 per day plus expenses for estate appraisals and consulting work, and $200 per hour for labor on handmade platinum jewelry work at the bench. Both involved working under a microscope. If every other single financial asset that I owned had disappeared, I could still have made a darned good living on either of those skills alone. Fortunately, several other investments made more money than that. Most of it was passive income to one degree or another. The high paid skills are what will help you get started quicker on your journey to wealth, and then are always there any time you need them to sustain you through a rough stretch.

Develop at least one high income skill.

CHAPTER 100

SAVE ONE OUNCE OF SILVER EVERY WEEK

This is the last lesson, but is one of the most important ones.

If you ignored every other thing in this book and did only this one thing, you will be on your way to becoming wealthy. It would be much, much slower and foolish to ignore all the other lessons in this book, but this one lesson alone would get you to your seed money in a little over a decade. If you did this alone and chose to ignore most of the other lessons in this book, you wouldn't make millionaire status by age 30, but you might do it by age 45. Of course, it is best to use everything you learned together from these 100 lessons. If you do, and you do all of it faithfully, you WILL be a millionaire by age 30.

Silver has been used throughout history along with gold as a financial instrument of value and a basis for coinage. Unlike contrived paper money, it has an intrinsic value backing the money as well as a commercial industrial commodity value. It is vital in the computer age and in the solar age. It was the basis of U.S. coinage until 1965 when the Federal government started to debase the coinage in circulation by removing the silver from it. Our wonderful country has gotten incrementally weaker since then.

The current price of silver is +/- $18 per ounce for pure silver on the spot market which means the actual price of the metal without a small dealer commission.

Silver can be purchased in a standardized and recognizable increment. It can be purchased in one troy ounce coins, called silver eagles issued by the US Mint. Each coin contains exactly one troy ounce of PURE silver. (Stay away from the private mint issues such as the Franklin Mint and many others who are even less known). Silver eagles are considered a silver bullion coin which is primarily valued for the silver content alone. Some collectors will collect top grade NGC or PCGS certified coins in sealed plastic holders and will pay considerable premiums for the possibility of increased collector's value. I have done both, but for financial accumulation alone I prefer generic, non-certified silver eagles. I usually buy them in 500 ounce lots in a sealed green colored box called a "monster box" with mint seal straps still on the box. You can buy any quantity from one single coin to plastic tubes of twenty coins. For smaller quantities than a monster box, you will pay a little more dealer's premium above spot price for each coin.

Previous to 1964, all silver coinage in the U.S. was made of 90% silver. I also buy bags of 90% circulated silver dollars, half dollars, quarters, and dimes because they are also recognizable and of specific weights. Stay away from 40% silver coins which were minted after 1963.

Although I do have some pure silver bars, I don't recommend them. They aren't as easily negotiable as coins. Coin dealers and metals dealers will always buy coins for immediate cash.

I highly recommend that you invest in at least one ounce of silver per week, as consistently as you breathe. That will be an investment of about $21 per week and you won't even miss it. This small increment is palatable for anyone.

I won't get into all of the details, but the silver market and gold markets have been manipulated by the crooked banking system for several years. When it all catches up with them, and it will, both metals will soar in price to reflect their real value as compared to paper money. They have been held artificially low for several years with the ignorance or tacit approval of some crooked politicians.

Right now, J.P.Morgan, Goldman Sacks, and other large banks are accumulating millions of ounces of physical silver (much of it in silver eagles) at these very low prices. Some have been charged with manipulating the market by the Federal Government and are being fined millions of dollars for doing so. In my opinion, even though fines are in the millions of dollars, they just consider the fines a nuisance, pay them, and keep on manipulating the metals because the payoff will eventually be enormous. They originally held and sold paper promissory certificates called "paper silver". They dumped the paper certificates onto unsophisticated public investors so they, themselves, could start accumulating the real physical metal instead of the paper promises that could become irredeemable. The people with the paper certificates will likely lose all of their money when the prices start to run and physical silver is demanded for payment. Never, never buy paper certificates guaranteeing delivery in actual physical silver. ALWAYS BUY AND HOLD PHYSICAL SILVER ONLY. Later, you might also want to hold gold. Same thing applies—ONLY BUY AND HOLD THE PHYSICAL METAL.

Accumulate your silver until you have your seed money, and then put it to work. I have never stopped accumulating silver. It is always immediately convertible to large chunks of cash to take advantage of any other investment that presents itself. I have repeatedly used silver to convert to chunks of ready cash when I needed it several times for a business deal which had even more opportunity.

If you are working a job for hourly pay, add any raises you earn toward your silver stash before you get accustomed to spending it. Buy whatever ounces the raise will pay for. If you don't get accustomed to spending the extra money from a raise, you will never miss it. Your initial investment will grow by leaps and bounds. You will cut years off the time it takes to get your seed money. Remember that when you buy silver, you haven't spent the money. You have converted one form of money (paper) that loses its purchasing power into another form of money (precious metal) that doesn't lose its purchasing power. It is a very good investment in itself. You have saved it, and it has potential of increasing value. The upside potential of owning silver today is much greater than the downside potential. That is how you measure all investments. Cash out the silver only when an even better immediate business opportunity arises.

Save one ounce of silver every week.

IN CONCLUSION

I HAVE TOLD YOU EXACTLY HOW TO BECOME A MILLIONAIRE BY AGE 30

NOW IT IS UP TO YOU. IF YOU REALLY WANT TO BE WEALTHY BAD ENOUGH, YOU WILL DO IT.

IF YOU ARE TOO LAZY TO READ AND DO WHAT IS NECESSARY, YOU WILL LIVE A LESSER LIFE THAN YOU COULD HAVE LIVED.

To my beloved grandchildren: BELIEVE IN YOURSELF!!!

Love,

Grandpa

IMPORTANT FURTHER READING

There are many books that are useful in helping you improve yourself to become more successful. The ones listed here are the ones that I have personally found to be the most beneficial to me.

LEAD THE FIELD	by Earl Nightingale	paperback from Amazon	$11
SEE YOU AT THE TOP	by Zig Ziglar	" " "	$13
RICHEST MAN IN BABYLON	by George S. Clason	" " "	$20
WINNING THROUGH INTIMIDATION	by Robert Ringer	" " "	$8
LOOKING OUT FOR #1	by Robert Ringer	" " "	$10
THINK AND GROW RICH	by Napoleon Hill	" " "	$12
THE MAGIC OF THINKING BIG	by David J. Schwartz	" " "	$10
THE POWER OF POSITIVE THINKING	by Dr. Norman Peale	" " "	$16
THE NEGOTIATING GAME	by Chester L. Karrass	" " "	$10
RICH DAD POOR DAD	by Robert T. Kiyosaki	" " "	$6
HOW TO WIN FRIENDS AND INFLUENCE PEOPLE	by Dale Carnegie	" " "	$15
THE MILLIONAIRE NEXT DOOR	by Thomas J. Stanley, Ph.D. and William D. Danko, Ph.D.	" " "	$6

Total $137

For $137 you can purchase literally millions of dollars of the best ideas and council that is available in the world. Each author has his own specific ideas, and they are all good. Some overlap, and some are unique. Learn from them all. If you make these books your guideline for living, you absolutely will become a successful person, and YOU WILL BE a millionaire.

THESE MEN WILL CHANGE YOUR LIFE

Printed in the United States
By Bookmasters